Walk-Ins
Soul Exchange

Karyn K. Mitchell, N.D., Ph.D

Walk-Ins/Soul Exchange by Karyn K. Mitchell N.D., Ph.D

Walk-Ins/Soul Exchange

Library of Congress Cataloging-in-Publication Data
Mitchell, Karyn
Walk-Ins/Soul Exchange
ISBN 0-9640822-4-1
1. Metaphysics 2. Psychology
94-075679

Copyright ©1999 by Karyn Mitchell

Cover by Robert Tentinger

Printed in the United States of America

1 2 3 4 5 6 7 8 9 10 11 12

The information in this book is for educational purposes only.

Walk-Ins/Soul Exchange by Karyn K. Mitchell N.D., Ph.D

Table of Contents

Foreword

Karyn has written a book that speaks to my soul! These accounts of past lives and Walk-Ins are so well documented that, while reading her book, I felt as if I was actually there in her office. I cried, and I laughed, and I felt many of the feelings that each person encountered. I also read this book with a rare fervor, earnestly turning each page. I couldn't wait to find out what the last session revealed. The outcome of each client was not what I could have predicted. The results were surprisingly perfect.

Karyn has a unique and exciting way of helping her readers to understand those situations that others have rarely tried to explain. She has brought together information that will not just encourage thought, and provoke new ideas, but help you to understand more than you asked in the beginning.

For me there is a truth that resonates throughout these pages from one encounter to the next. You can feel Karyn's careful guidance as her clients begin to share, understand and then heal their lives. This healing comes about in part because Karyn is a person who will step aside, abandoning her own interest, to allow another person to grow. Regardless if you agree with these experiences, her unselfish guidance and support is undeniable.

In my opinion Karyn has helped to build a bridge to a place very few people will admit exist.

By Tami Gramont, Writer

Prologue

I feel that I have been composing this book for an entire lifetime. The actual commitment to paper began in the year 1994. It is the culmination of spontaneous information gained from actual cases during the ten years that I have been involved in Age Regression Therapy. In my work I never once set out to discover that Walk-Ins do exist on our planet. Neither did I ever ask that such information be revealed to me in any way during the course of therapy work. I was actually quite surprised and a bit taken aback whenever such information unraveled itself in the following sessions that I share with you. Most of the cases that I have encountered involving exchanged souls seem to be complex at the very least. Many of these individuals have very little memory of their childhood experiences, and relate that what they do think they "remember" are actually events that others told them about. Another commonality is the revelation that there were difficult times such as a major physical or emotional trauma, often followed by a type of physical, emotional, mental, and even spiritual reeducation or reevaluation. The experience is much like a Shamanic Death followed by a dramatic Spiritual Rebirth. I have heard it said that it is by going through the fire that one learns what really matters in life. Many times the Walk-In becomes a bit of an anathema to those who knew them as the old self. Family members and friends are often dismayed at the radical change in their re-birthed loved one. A Walk-In often becomes the black sheep in the family and is criticized and perhaps even ostracized if their beliefs differ from the status quo. A Walk-In never really feels that they fit in with the rest of society, or truly feel at home anywhere, even in the body that they inhabit. One Walk-In mentioned that he felt as if he was wearing a pair of shoes that were one size too big.

To some extent, we are all Walk-Ins...souls who drift into a life seeking to achieve our Soul's Purpose. However, the experiences that I share with you in this book are revelations by people who entered into a previously occupied body; a life that represents a work already in progress. I feel from these experiences and others that I choose not to share, that many of these souls have entered at this particular time for an important reason. I also feel that many of the Walk-Ins are unaware of their ultimate purpose or the destined outcome of their role in the history of this planet. They seem content to follow steadfastly, without question, the brief course set before them. It is ironic that many of these souls are delivering the same ageless message in different tongues, in different bodies, on different continents, in divergent cultures through various religions and symbols; have done this and continue to do this throughout human history. And even before that. A Walk-In dares ask the question "From whence to where." But the answer and the message that they deliver is always the same. The message is...Love and Life are Eternal.

Common Characteristics of A Walk-In Soul

1.) Seem to have missing memories of their childhood.
2.) Generally do not have an easy time in early life.
3.) Have a great reverence for life.
4.) Do not fear their own physical death.
5.) Are driven throughout their life to find their purpose or serve in some way.
6.) Become aware of simultaneous and past lifetimes.
7.) Are detached for the most part from unnecessary drama.
8.) Become aware that they create their own reality, including their exit from life.
9.) Abhor the suffering of any lifeform.
10.) Generally feel lonely and out of place with other people.
11.) Are non-violent and abhor violence of any kind.

Walk-In

And so the odyssey begins again. Tethered to our physical bodies like ancient, weathered balloons, we return to Earth to experience life and kiss death once again. Some choose to birth as a door. Others, like the mythical Persephone, enter a darkened world and merge like springtime with a body bereft of magic and passion. Spirit-born free of the womb. There is a mission. There is always a mission. However, the nature and essence of that mission is rarely revealed until the soul's light has been properly calibrated to fit the essence of Earth Energies. This is the timing mechanism that activates when the Walk In begins to "awaken." This magnetic "clock" is a simplification of the process, and there is much more involved than is easily understood. Each Soul Exchange experience is different, and sometimes unusual or unlikely. Generally, the soul that is incoming must first complete the active karma initiated by the natal soul before the mission begins.

I had heard years ago that it was believed that the great achievers, the historical figures throughout time were Walk-ins; such souls as Anwar Sadat. who, alone in his prison cell, called out in despair to be released of his physical bondage. After that cry was answered, his Earthly mission was then continued with renewed vigor by a Mahatma, or "Great Soul," who traded places with the natal soul, the soul born in the body. While it is compelling to want to believe that only the most evolved Mahatmas or even the "old" souls are capable of soul exchange, I make no such judgment concerning the circumstances of soul exchange in general, nor of the individual souls or cases here involved. I do not personally believe that in all cases soul exchanges are prearranged, as some of these accounts may illustrate. Whether it is pure chance or the Transcendental notion of fate, I feel that there may be a broader plan or purpose at work than we may realize or recognize.

It may be difficult for readers to relate to the notion that soul exchange is even possible. There are often accounts in Shamanism where a traumatized individual may lose part of their soul in the event or encounter with near death or great fear. A "Soul Recovery" is then done to retrieve the fragmented parts of the traumatized soul. There are also stories of Hindu Yogis who practice "Parakaya Pravesha," an advanced technique where a yogi casts off the body at will and acquires another body as he or she chooses. There are accounts of war prisoners who apparently willed their souls with their mind to leave or completely evacuate the body to escape their prison. Astral travel is similar but not always a willed occurrence. As Shakespeare once said, "There is more to Heaven and Earth, Horatio, than man has ever dreamed of..."

Note to reader: All names have been changed in these accounts. All names are entirely fictitious.
Karyn Mitchell, Earth Year 1999

Dreaming of Life

You hold a smoldering dream gently in the palm of your hand
It whispers, "open your palm, give me birth, let me live"
But you are afraid of dreaming and hide it in your pocket, deep.
Someday, maybe, you will draw it into the sunlight, out.

And then it happened. The dawn of spirit essence, yearning
Free to be, it is time. Know that what is real
You have hidden from yourself, buried it alive.
It breathes there still. Feel it now stirring softly.

A fire-filled dragon in my sleep, this dream becomes the mist
Of life's essence, surrounding, caressing, teaching gently
That you are not that dispassionate dreamer, but the smoldering Dream
Waiting for the sweet kiss of life's longing to begin.

by Karyn Mitchell

Door at Wells Cathedral
Photo by Shauna Angel Blue

A Holocaust Soul As Walk-In

"They shot her! She was crawling ahead of me in the frozen grass. I had just cleared the barbed wire around the camp when I saw the lights turn on her. Then I heard the shots." Piotr begins to cry softly. "I can't believe it. I've got to get to her. She's not moving." He jumps to his feet and runs forward toward the body crumpled in the tall grass. Two more shots pierce the quiet fall night. He falls and inches his way on his belly to his beloved Sonia, pulling himself with the frozen grass. His hands are bleeding. He lifts her head and feels the cool absence of her soul. There is no breath. An icy shudder, then a searing pain goes down his spine. She is standing there, above him, looking down with a sweet, serene smile upon her face. He cannot comprehend what is happening, why he sees her there. "Get down", he yells. Why is she smiling? She has not smiled in months. His legs are numb and lifeless as he tries to stand to join her. He falls hard to the frozen winter ground. He feels something warm and wet running down his arm. Two bullets have lodged deep in his back, one in the mid-spine, the other in his right kidney perhaps. Focusing only upon her, he has failed to notice that he is silently bleeding to death. He hears the Nazi soldiers running toward them. Closer. "Get down!" He yells to her. He hears one more shot. Then he hears nothing. But she is still standing there, now holding out her hand for him. He tries to lift himself once again, to reach for her. This time it is easy, effortless. They are free of their bodies. Their bodies lie on the frozen earth. The soldiers are kicking at them. The bodies are lifeless. They join hands and walk deep into the interior of the death camp of Auschwitz-Birkenau where they believe that their family members are being held. For him there was his mother, his father, and his younger sister. For her it was her father and mother who were taken, and before that, her older brother. They were out together when the raid took place. They pledged to liberate their loved ones or die together trying. They are going to complete their mission. They now search quietly among the suffering life forms to detect any sign of their *missing relatives. She is still there, searching. I am no longer there."*

And now she is searching for him as well. He was taken, forced into another body, another life-in-progress. This is his own true story...as a Holocaust Victim as a reluctant Walk-In.

> *"Some die without having really lived,*
> *while others continue to live,*
> *in spite of the fact that they have died."*
> Author unknown

We begin at the beginning...

"I keep having this dream, this nightmare." Todd was a twenty-three year old professional, deeply depressed, casual in his day-off gray cotton sweater and faded blue jeans.

Such begins the most incredible account I have ever heard. "Tell me about the dream," I reply, leaning forward with my clipboard with paper blank scripted only with the date, name, and session number: Todd Robbins, Mar. 11, 1994, Session 1.

He continued, "I've been looking for the same woman since I was seventeen. I call her my 'dream woman.' She has brown hair, shoulder length cut, brown eyes, and the most...loving smile you could imagine."

"Have you seen her somewhere before? Outside of your dreams I mean?"

"No...Yes. I don't know. She's just there, smiling. I love her. I know that. It is the one thing that I am sure of. I think..." He paused and chewed his lower lip. "I feel that I have trouble with relationships because no one measures up to her. Or at least what I think. I just can't go on like this. Lately I can't sleep, I can't eat, all I do is think about her. That's why I called you. You do regression work, and I think that's what I need maybe. I don't know. I'm so confused, obsessed, that I don't even know who I am anymore."

"And you feel that a regression might help you understand your frequent dreams about this mystery woman."

"Yes. That's what I want. But there is something else." He took a sip of his water. "I have always felt that my parents aren't really my parents, like someone else might be their son, not me. I don't feel that bond, I just don't belong with them. I feel like I just woke up one day in this house with strangers. When I tried to tell them, they thought I had amnesia. It really happened that way. I feel like I was adopted in my teens, like I belong in another place or time."

Soon our regression therapy session began. I made no judgments about Todd's story, and simply decided to allow Todd's subconscious mind to take him back to the time "that the reason for his problems exist." Sometimes the simplest request can create the most complicated revelations. He related the following experience of Sonia and Piotr in Nazi Germany during World War Two. My first instinct was that Todd's experience involved classic Past-life trauma. However, that was not the case at all. There was more. Much more. Within seconds into the session, Todd began to hyperventilate. This is what his subconscious mind revealed:

"I sense other energy, this cold energy field moving toward us. It is foreign, something new. I don't know how long we've been searching in this death camp. Everything feels hollow, empty. I can't feel anything or smell anything or touch anything. I am just drifting around like smoke, looking...searching for my relatives. Then I see them. Sonia doesn't for some reason. They come directly toward me. Funny looking creatures with big heads, black eyes with no pupils, and bluish-gray transparent-looking skin. The hands are part of the arm with three long fingers and a thumb of sorts, maybe. They want me to come with them. Not without Sonia I say. But they don't seem to hear me. I cry out to her as they take me, paralyze me, manipulate me, in some sort of hold, trance."

I had to ask that Todd disassociate from the experience as it was creating a great deal of fear and panic. He was still hyperventilating a bit. In a few moments he went right back to the critical event...right back to the interior of an entirely metal room, he thought perhaps a ship where he indicated that he was compressed in a sort of clear glass-like holding tank.

"I can see a body on the metal table in front of me. Black hair, gray tee-shirt, dark blue denim looking pants...probably a teenager. Oh my, oh my..." he begins to moan. "It's me! It's this body! The body is this one. But I'm not in the body. I'm watching in the tank. I know that that body is not me, not mine! I'm watching them do things to that body, hooking up wires, tubes of some sort, feeding it. Feeding the brain too through a clear tube. The body looks very dead, lifeless. I know that the soul is gone. I know what death looks like by now. I saw it in the camps. Saw the souls fly out of the body. Liberated. But they've done something to the soul. It left the body, the soul did. Unexpected like. They seem mad about it leaving before they wanted it to. Before the body died. But they're not those cruel Nazi doctors. This messed them up. They're telling me this now, their story about the boy's soul leaving in the middle of one of their experiments. I'm to go into the body so they don't caught, don't get into trouble with someone or something. They're covering up for their mistake. But I don't want to! That's not me! They're attaching a tube to the glass container. Hooking it up to the back of the boy's head. No! I feel myself draining out. Going in...into the boy's body! No! Sonia...Sonia...I need to be with Sonia..." Piotr's thread-bare voice fades into eventual silence."

"Todd...Todd, are you all right?" He was sobbing, his body shaking in anguish.

"Who?" He responded in a breath broken in crying. "Todd who?"

"What is your name?" I don't quite yet understand what has transpired in nearly two minutes of complete silence. The thought of spirit possession entered my mind.

"I'm...Piotr. My name is Piotr."

"Piotr, how old are you?"

"I'm twenty. Where's my...where's Sonia? What have you done with her!?"

"Piotr, I want you to look around. Where are you? What do you see?"

"Strange room. He chokes a bit to catch his breath. Colored pictures on the entire wall. Soft blue rug on the floor. Window open. I see a lake, water, outside. Strange room...I've never seen anything like it before in Amsterdam. It's all new, so big. A funny white, window thing on the desk with keys like an English typewriter, but flat. A thin, black box with a thick lid and a wire coming from it. I hear something. Steps. Someone is coming!" He panics. "But not coming hard, like soldiers... coming in soft and quiet like." He grows still. It's a woman with dark, short hair. She is talking to me like she knows me. Touching my face. I don't like it. I don't know her. I stare at her and move back away on the bed. ` Am I hungry?' No. Why does this woman want to know if I am hungry? Late? Go where? I don't know any Jason, why would I go there? My head hurts...ohhh. The room is spinning, out of control. I'm losing consciousness. I tell her to get out. I'm sick!" He lifts his head and it wobbles back and forth. "My head!" He puts his left hand on the back of his head. "My head is going to explode..." He drops his head helplessly on the pillow.

"Listen," I said. "I'm going to count from one to three, and you will be just beyond this, just beyond this time. One, two, three! You are just beyond this! Take a deep breath now, releasing any pain that you might be holding onto. Breathe blue light into the pain and exhale any darkness. Breathe in blue and breathe out darkness and pain. Let it go." I can tell that he is feeling more comfortable. "It's time to come back now, come back to the present time, back to this room. Collect all of your thoughts, all of your energy, and prepare to come back feeling better than before, better than when we started. I'm going to count from one to ten and you will be back in this room, feeling better and better with each number, each breath. Remembering everything and allowing more to come to you at the most appropriate time when you're ready for it." I count him back into the reality of the present, the now. Our session took fifty minutes and spanned a half a century. I helped him to sit up slowly.

After a few moments I asked him, "How do you feel, Todd?"

I could tell that he was deep in thought, his brows furrowed. "I don't know. I don't know what to feel."

We discussed some of the events that occurred in the session, and especially his feelings about what he remembered. He stated that he was far too logical to believe that his experience held a place in his reflection of reality. He wanted to continue what we had started, and so we set an appointment for the following week. I encouraged him to just let his concerns for the validity of his experience to go, and allow his thoughts to flow to him. I encouraged him to keep a journal of his thoughts and feelings, and even to note his dreams. I told him that what was most important was the emotional content of his reaction to the experience. In short, I asked him not to judge but to free himself to feel.

Todd seemed more depressed than ever when I next saw him. He looked tired, drained. I helped him settle into the big couch and brought a cup of chamomile tea to him. He was cold from his trip and said that the heater in his car was not working properly. "Like my life. It's just like my life. Nothing's working," he said. "I feel like a lost cause."

"But you have to trust that things will work out. There is a saying from a writer named Og Mandino: 'This too shall pass.' When we feel down, we think that it will always be that way. But things change. We have the power to change and create what we want in our lives. Things will get better. Sometimes it's like a switch that we flip and everything gets lighter and life goes our way. Other times it's a slower process. But it is a process. Trust the process. You will feel better. You have to know that in your heart." I noticed that he had on the same gray sweater and faded blue jeans that he had on last week. I wondered if he had changed his clothes. "Tell me how your week has been, Todd."

"I've still been dreaming about her." "Sonia," he mutters.

"Sonia...Sonia from your regression?" I looked at him deeply, feeling his despair, his pain.

"She comes to me every night now, or most every night in dreams. I see her face more clearly now. So serious."

I noticed that he had come into my office without notes or a notebook. I knew that he had not journaled, nor had he intended or wanted to. I could not blame him for his apathy or lack of compliance. Depressed people are often too overwhelmed to do much of anything except vital functions. "Todd, what do you think her visits mean? Does she ever communicate with you?"

"I told you. I've been looking for her for years. And don't call me Todd. I don't like that name anymore. I am not this..." He grabs the gray sweater and pulls hard, out on the vee. "Not this...Todd." I hear an accent now, suddenly a heavy, foreign accent, spoken in English but with disdain of the very words, the language.

In our last session, it had briefly occurred to me that perhaps Todd might be "possessed" by another soul or entity. This sudden accent might reveal a possession of some sort or even the thought of M.P.D., Multiple Personality Disorder, crossed my mind. I decided to engage this personality, whomever it might be. "Then tell me more about yourself. More about who you really are."

"I'm not sure I want to tell you." Now I realize the disdain of the language and also a hint of disdain for me. He thought I was indulging him. But I knew that he knew he still needed my help. And that bothered him more than anything.

"Are you angry about something?"

"Angry?! Angry?! Did my...the woman who calls herself my mother...did she call you? He slammed himself back into the couch."

"No. Was she going to?" I relaxed back into the cushion of my chair, balancing his reaction.

"Hell yes I'm mad. 'Angry.' Wouldn't you be? Don't you get it? This is NOT my body. I'm telling you. This is not me! I don't know who I am!" The accent was thick and real.

"So. What do you think has really happened to you?"

He glared at me. His face was flushed with anger and confusion. He brought his hands up to his face and pulled them down. There were tears. His body started to shake. "You know..." he whispered. "You know. There is no other explanation. I don't believe it either." Was that accent Polish, German, or Dutch? He couldn't hide it now. It was a part of him.

"So, what do you feel we should do in our session today?" I asked. "How can I most help you?" I wanted him to know that I was sincere in my desire to help him find his truth. He kept staring forward in silence, mesmerized. I continued. "In the case of trauma, I generally try to assist my clients in finding as many relevant background details as possible to verify or...affirm events. Especially if the client is... hesitant or reluctant to accept what might have happened. If the details fit the events, that helps with clarification. It verifies your experience, or doesn't."

He continued to stare blankly at the thread of moving traffic outside the window. A window which revealed only about eight inches of life between the close-drawn shade. I knew he'd heard me. "I want to know about Sonia. Details about Sonia. I just want to know more about Sonia. I don't know if I want more about other things." I knew that he was struggling with the surreal aspects of his last regression. Alien beings forcing him into this foreign body. It would be a bit difficult for any person to accept.

"Of course." I said. I could sense his fear. "Are you sure you're ready for another regression?" I asked. "We could wait."

"Wait for what?" he snapped. "I need to know more. I need to understand a few things. My...mother, Mrs. Robbins, tells me I cannot come back...home until I lose this anger. I think she's afraid of me. Of the anger." He moved sideways on the couch. "I have been unhappy and more than a bit loud at home. I yelled at her to leave me alone. I told her I didn't know her. That she wasn't my mother. Oh yeah, they've drug me to shrinks before. I know what you're thinking. Nothing. I just didn't remember. Amnesia they said. Thousands of dollars in therapy because I couldn't remember our vacation in Disneyland when I was ten." He started to laugh sarcastically. "Details. Yes. I'm ready for some details, whether it's Sonia or Disneyland. Let's go." We moved to the quieter space of the second therapy room.

We were ten minutes into the regression when Todd started to speak in another language. Perhaps French or Dutch I decided. I had forgotten to give the general directive to speak only in English. I heard the words "Andre. De faculteit en medische neurobiologie. Then the word Uv A, then the word Singel." It seemed that he was in the middle of a conversation.

I asked, "Are you alone now or with someone?" He ignored me. The dialogue continued. "I ask that you speak only in English now. Speak English." And he did. I wanted him to continue his dialogue, but the conversation had stopped. "Where are you?"

"We are leaving the library complex on Singel. By the Militia Building now. I've hired a carrel for three months while I work on my thesis. It's really hard." he stops.

"What is hard?" I want him to continue.

"It's my fifth year. Working on my Master's Degree at the University van Amsterdam. Economics. It's so hard. I'm burned out. From my studies, from what is happening here. One by one our rights are taken from us. He laughs. Even whom we can have sexual intercourse with. Stars. Badges. Registration. I'm glad to see Sonia. She's always so...optimistic. She cheers me up. She asks me if I've heard about Professor Andre, somebody who teaches at the medical school here. It's November, and there's a tour going through. New students and their parents. We stop talking. The parents, mostly Dutch, look at us like we're dirt. They know we're Jewish because of the 'Jood.' The badge. There are none in the tour. It seems so hopeless to start new things. And there is no money."

She is telling me more, whispering, as people pass by, something like, "They say he was shipped to Mauthausen... the camp in Austria with a couple hundred other men, who ignored the edicts of Seyss-Inquart. He said that the Nazis would respect Dutch ideology." She laughed aloud. "For years their puppet Arthur has been issuing new edicts against us in the 'Het Joodchse Weekblad.' We think he's dead, the professor." Then there was silence followed by fragmented phrases. Political in nature, about Queen Wilhelmina in London, and 'De Vonk' news. Hitler blames the Jewish people for the German defeat in World War One. The NSB is mentioned twice.

Details. What details. "I want you to tell me everything that you know about Sonia."

"Her family moved here, to Amsterdam, just after the Kristallnacht in Berlin. 1938. They burned her synagogue and sent thousands to camps. After that Holland started to close down to immigrants like a lot of other countries. The depression hit here late. Tough times. No jobs for those who moved here. They thought Holland was a safe place. She had an uncle, Aaron Stein, living here who had a clothing business. He assured them. They got on a waiting list to the United States. Could take two years. They would wait. She had studied nursing in Berlin, but did not get to finish her studies. Here they are poor. Her brother had to sign on to a work camp called Westerbork. He does not write anymore. They are afraid for him. Maybe he's sick." He sighs lightly.

"Tell me about you. About your family. What is your name?"

"I am Piotr. Piotr Cohen. My father is Jacob Cohen, one of the directors on the Jewish Council. My mother's name is Eva. We live in an apartment in Centrum, Keizergracht 140...on the canal. Not far from West Church. I grew up there with my sister and mother and father. It's the only home I know. The apartment building is really narrow when you look up at it from the street. It is a mustard color, connected to a whole row of narrow buildings, built in the 17th century, each one a different color. I love the designs on the outside of the these buildings. We have a kind of curved feather design on the outside of ours. There are stairs, two flights. Our place is nice, but I hear a rumor that we must move soon. There is a German family that wants our apartment, we got a letter from someone named Asscher. My mother is worried. People she knows are disappearing. People who registered but refused to show up to the work camps when they heard what was happening there. No one hears from them again. Rumor has it they are murdered or worked to death. We have two months to find a place to move. My father is protesting to the Council. They are 'sympathetic,' but in the same situation. My father's brother, Henri, committed suicide after the capitulation of Holland to the Third Reich. He had no wife or children to worry about. I think he was smart. He doesn't have to worry or live this nightmare of wondering and fear." His accent is thick, just as it was before.

"Piotr, I want you to go to the most important event that you shared with Sonia," I said.

"We are walking back from the University. I've completed a lot of research and I feel better about it. We feel it first. Something is wrong. Really wrong. We go through town, the market. Windows are broken. No one is there. We look at each other. It's like we know. I don't want her to go home alone, but I want to know about my family. I go with her. The pan is burned dry on the stove. It smells. She runs from room to room. Only small things are gone, like people could carry. But some things are wrecked, like a bureau smashed and drawers missing. We know. She slides to the floor and screams. I try to quiet her. They might come back. 'They might be out there still, quiet yourself Sonia!' It is getting darker outside. 'Come with me. I have to go home. I have to know.' But she won't move, won't stop crying. Finally, I run out into the street, looking up the street and then down. To the canal, Keizergracht. Up the steps. Gone, just like hers. I yell for them. 'Mother!' 'Father!' Her sweater is gone from the back of the chair. Their coats. The silence strangles me. But there! A note. A piece of paper dropped on the table. From my mother. Two words. 'Goodse Schouwgurg'. The Theater. They were told where they were going. I run to the Theater. Crowds of people huddled, afraid, inside. NSB, the Dutch Nazis, bullying them. But they aren't there. I don't see them. I am watching outside for hours, hiding. I listen to the talk, some in German, some in Dutch. These people are being transported to Sobibor, a camp somewhere. I hear that from a member of the NSB who is talking outside. The people don't know what will happen. In two days, at Sobibor they will be exterminated, murdered, immediately when they get there. Preparations are made. Orders given. Papers are being signed now by those inside. Signing away their possessions, their life. I am horrified, afraid for my family. I don't know where to look now. I don't know where they went. I move closer to the window. A friend of my mother's, Rachel, sees me in the window. Her eyes get big. She is afraid for me. For them all. Nervous, wringing her old hands. She shakes her head, no, and then looks away quickly. Not there. They've taken them somewhere else. But where? I'm alone. I think of all of the places where they could be detained for questioning. If only Father had not registered us! Compliant. I am angry at him for always doing what he was told. Like sheep. They all registered. It was a matter of faith in...Holland. No, not Holland, not my country. It was our very own Arthur... He had betrayed us all. Betrayed us to the Nazis. Lying to us all the while. His own people. Then I think of Sonia. No. I look again. Her parents are not there either. They're not going to Sobibor either. There's a chance. But Sonia doesn't know. Sonia alone too, in her flat. I move away quietly from there, and then I run back into town. She has fallen asleep on the floor, face and hair wet with tears. It must be midnight. I hear the central bell sounding, I count. I look out of the window. The snow is falling, soft and white. Peaceful. I wake her up. I explain to her that we might find them. They are not going to Sobibor! They will live. They are alive. We can rescue them and then flee Holland. There are people I know in the Council. In the morning we will find them if they are not gone also. We rip the badges off our jackets. We have a plan. We wait for morning, sometimes sleeping but mostly not." I am holding her against me.

The floor is very hard and cold. She is all I have left of my old life. That charade of a life. But we are alive."

It has been almost an hour. I know that the session must end now. I ask one final question. "Piotr, what year is it?" I wait.

""The year?" He repeats. "It is 1943. I am to graduate next spring."

I direct him to come back, remembering everything. I have taped the session. Taped the details. Too many details. We both know that there are too many details. He sits up and I ask him how he feels. He has that faraway look that I often see when a client returns to the present after a long session. He says nothing. I get him a glass of water which he now holds, reflecting. We make small talk as he prepares to leave.

Thursday already. I look at the schedule. The week has passed quickly. I draw out Todd's file. Read the volume of notes scribbled after the last session. I am always careful with my notes. I never write real notes about alien abduction experiences. I use a code or references that only I know. Just enough to jog the memory. I know we must go on if he is ready. How would I feel if I were him? I always ask myself that question. It doesn't help. I am horrified by the events of the Holocaust. Those details. I keep staring at the year, the date: 1943. I have researched some of the statistics. Over six million Jewish people, men, women, and children were exterminated by the Nazis in World War II. A gas called Zyclon B was used in the showers. And perhaps those were the lucky ones. The horrors of the medical experimentation, starvation, soul-breaking abuse, and being worked to the very death of the human body. I look up from my notes and see his black Mercedes drive into the parking lot.

As Todd settles in on the couch, I ask him how his week has been. He has come directly from work and has on a dark suit jacket, white shirt, and tie. Very corporate. He stands, takes off the jacket, loosens and pulls off his tie, dropping them both on the couch. He sits down again. "On automatic pilot," he smiles at me. "I'm just doing what I have to do, no more, no less." His voice is flat.

"Would you like some tea or water?" I ask.

"Tea would be great." He continues as I bring him the Chamomile tea. "I've been doing some thinking though, and I'm not so angry anymore. Just kind of...numb. No feelings about anything. Apathetic. One of the 'strategies' that I learned from one of the psychiatrists that I saw when I was seventeen was to identify or classify as many different types of feelings that I would experience every day. I came up with only two: apathy and anger. He said that I was not experiencing the full range of human emotions. We did word/emotion association. Apathy and anger. That was it. Now that the anger is absent for the present, there is only apathy left." He sipped his tea, detached.

"Was it because you were seventeen? A teenager's response to the world?" I smiled at him.

"No. It's still and always has been the same as long as I know."

That statement was significant, as long as I know...I thought about it. I asked him about dreams. There were none. Lots of work, he said, too exhausted when he finally got to bed. "What do you do at work?" I had been curious.

"I establish computer systems for companies. I work for my father." He sat back. "I am not that computer literate. Technology confuses me."

"But, do you like what you do?"

"It's a job, that's all." He seemed...apathetic. Better than angry, I thought.

It was not long before we were back in Amsterdam. Fifty years in less than fifteen minutes. The mind is powerful in its intention to assist the body and spirit on its healing journey through time. He continues:

"We are careful. Everyone is being taken that they can find. We find out that a group was recently shipped to Auschwitz-Birkenau via train. We are led to believe that they are on it. I get my father's map. We will follow the tracks to Amersfoot, down the Rhine to Frankfort, to Prague, and then to Oweicium. Poland. To Auschwitz." He shivered. "We will help them to escape. Sonia,

they will be all right." Then he is suddenly quiet. "Someone, a woman, is screaming. In the street. Running. Shots are fired. It's quiet again. We don't want to look but we do. We are glad that we don't know who it is. Sonia is crying. We have to get out of here! She asks me if I have ever seen anyone die before. She has, in the hospital once. She felt the spirit go right through her. She is afraid to die. I hold her. I tell her that she is not going to die. I won't let anything happen to her. We find scissors and cut her hair short, like a man's. She puts on a shirt and pair of my pants and a belt to pull them tight. We have the map, what food we can find, jacket and extra socks. We are ready to go. We make our way out of the city in the darkness and follow the tracks to Hilversum. We hide and sleep in the daylight. There have been two trains go by, cattle cars filled with our people. We watch as each car goes by, hoping to catch even a glimpse of our families, or clothing we might identify. Nothing. It is painful. It seems the cars themselves are moaning, but it is coming from inside. I am grateful when we reach the Rhine. I want to stay there for a day or two, but Sonia wants to go on. I have grown to appreciate and love her. We take care of each other, take turns sleeping and watching. We never feel safe, but we are alive. It seems like it has been a couple of months since we left Amsterdam. We are exhausted and hungry. We decide that we must find some food somewhere so that we can have strength to go on. We want to steal eggs from a farmyard, but it is deserted. We only find a part of a sack of moldy, ground corn. We take it with us, grateful." He falls silent.

"Piotr, what happens next?" I ask.

"We are there. At the field near the camp." His body jerks suddenly. "They shot her! She was crawling ahead of me, in the darkness, in the frozen prairie grass. I had just cleared the barbed wire when I saw the lights and heard the shots." He begins to cry softly. "I can't believe it. I've got to get to her. I jump to my feet and run forward toward the body crumpled on the grass. Two more shots pierce the quiet winter night. They shatter into my body, my back. But I don't feel them. I inch my way on my belly, pulling on the frozen grass, to my beloved Sonia. My hands are bleeding. I lift her head and feel the cool absence of her soul. There is no breath in her body. I kiss her, crying. Saying her name. Calling her back. An icy shudder goes down my spine. She is standing there, above me, looking down with a sweet, serene smile upon her face. I do not know what is happening, why I see her there. Why she is smiling. She has not smiled in months. My legs are numb and lifeless. I try to stand to join her. I fall hard on the frozen ground. I feel something cold and wet on my arm. Two bullets lodged deep in my back, one in the mid-spine, maybe the other in his right kidney. I hear shouts and soldiers running toward us. Focusing only upon her, I am getting very cold, silently bleeding to death. There is one more shot. I only hear it. Then there is only her. I try to lift himself once again, to reach for her. This time it is easy, effortless. I reach for her. We join hands and walk deep into the interior of the death camp. We will find and save our families. I will keep her safe."

In the next session, I began the regression by asking that Todd go back to the time that he needed to go to to learn what he needed to know. The subconscious mind understands such directions and generally takes us to the "critical event." His breathing grows more shallow and quickens. He grips the arm of the chair.

"No, no! I am not a disenfranchised soul. You have no right to do this to me! I've been captured, haven't I? This is just some Nazi joke or experiment or something. Get away from me! Where's Sonia? What have you done to her? Let me go!" He tries to move his hands, but it is as if someone is holding them down. He quiets for a moment, listening.

"Can you tell me what's happening?" I asked.

"This is unbelievable. I don't believe this! They are telling me what a great favor they are offering me. She/he...whatever it is, keeps telling me that I am 'sans manu', void of materiality, no form, no body to interact with the Third Dimension."

"What are they saying?"

"They are not speaking, like we speak. I am understanding what they may me to know. I am dead, and he...Todd is dead. Both two dead parts. I have no body and he has no soul. He left, and they...those things... forced me, my soul, into this body with their technology. Piotr, that's who I really am. Piotr Cohen of Amsterdam. An economics student. I am not Todd Robbins. He died on that table while the Aliens were conducting their experiments. I am told that I, I mean he, had terrible asthma and nosebleeds. I never had them in his body." His silence was a reflection of the deep emotional pain that his soul was experiencing. I realized that he must be homesick and filled with unresolved grief over his missing parents.

"Do you know how many years that you and Sonia wandered through that death camp?"

"I have no idea. We never found them. Never." He started to cry. "And now I am a prisoner in this other body. I do not even know where Sonia is."

I thought that perhaps another perspective might help him. "I want you to go just beyond this to a place where we can heal all of this. I ask that whoever and all that we need to help us heal be there as well. You are there now."

He was silent. For the next several minutes I knew that he was not alone wherever he was. It was as if he was listening to someone. Then his eyes opened slowly. He looked more at peace than he had ever been since I'd known him. There had been some sort of internal or cosmic reconciliation.

"How do you feel?" I asked.

"Better...much better." He replied. I handed him a glass of water. "Thanks."

"Do you want to talk about what happened to you?" I asked.

He cleared his throat a bit. "That was quite an experience." Todd replied. Then he was quiet again. Reflecting. He stood up. "If it's all right, I'd rather just digest this a bit. Until next week." He smiled as he left, and did appear more relaxed in his body.

Another week passed, and I was eager to hear how Todd was doing. He was on time as usual.

"You know," he began, "I am really grateful...that you have helped me to find the truth about all of this. I felt like I was mentally retarded all of this time. A step behind everyone else at school and running to catch up with it all."

"I can imagine how that might have affected you," I said. "Do you feel like you have any closure on this last part of your life?"

He laughed. It was good to see him laugh with sincere joy rather than with sarcasm. "And I thought you were going to ask me what I had learned from all of this. I was ready for that." He looked at his hands. The hands that belonged to Todd Robbins and now him. He had inherited them. "I have learned that I am grateful now for this new beginning of sorts. In a way, it's as if there was a big gap and now I am continuing my life. Like a twist on reincarnation, only born to a mature body instead of a baby. I am a living, breathing anachronism."

"Have you ever gotten used to it?" He stared at me with a blank look on his face. "The body. Todd's body. Did you ever get used to it?"

He thought for a moment. "Do you know what it is like to wear a pair of shoes that are one size too large for you? That's what it's been like. But I know that it, my 'amnesia,' has been hard for the Robbins family too. I never did understand. Until now. Our sessions explained the gap in my life. But I will not tell them, the Robbins, the truth about what happened to their son. They would only think that I was making all of this up, for one thing. And, for another," he sighed, "Well, I just don't have the heart to tell them that their son's soul, their son... has died. They just wouldn't buy any of it. I don't think this would fit anywhere into their Lutheran theology." He entwined his fingers. He was wearing a fraternity ring on his right hand. I never noticed a ring before. "It would be hard for anyone to believe, unless it happened to them. It was too real for me. I have no doubts."

"Do you think you will ever be able to, or want to tell anyone else what really happened to you?" I wondered.

"Well, maybe my wife one of these days..." he smiled. "But maybe not until after we're married," he teased.

It has been five years since I put the file of Todd Robbins away. As I sort the mail, I notice a thick envelope from the Hoffman Estates, Illinois. Inside is a photograph and a birth announcement:

> *"Todd and Tina Robbins proudly announce the birth of their daughter, Sonia Eva, born November 12 at 3:00 p.m. Seven Pounds, eight ounces..."*

There was a hand scripted note on the bottom of the white formal announcement from Todd:

I knew she was coming back to me. I met Tina at Synagogue. What a beautiful gift life is!
Thank You for helping me find myself.
Todd

> "What we call the end is also a beginning.
> The end is where we start from."
>
> T.S. Eliot

> "There is no end.
> There is no beginning. There is only the infinite passion of life."
>
> Federico Fellini

July 14, 1861

My very dear Elizabeth,

My love for you is deathless...but if I do not return, never forget how much I love you. And when my last breath escapes me on the battle field, it will whisper your name. But, Oh Elizabeth! If the dead can come back to this earth and flit unseen around those they have loved, I shall always be near you; in the gladdest days and the darkest nights, always, always. And if there be a soft breeze upon your cheek, it shall be my breath, as the cool air fans your throbbing temple, it shall be my spirit passing by. Elizabeth do not mourn me dead; think I am gone and wait for thee, for we shall meet again.

A Letter from Major Sullivan Ballou who died at the first battle of Bull Run

Personal Interview With a Walk-In

KM: Who are you? I know your name, but would like to know who you believe you are.

WI: And you also know I am a Walk-In from our years together.

KM: Yes.

WI: Well, as a Walk-In, I tend to view my life as a collection of past, present...which also includes simultaneous lifetimes, and future lives. I have experienced more than nine hundred single-life streams which can be best described as a string of pearls in a row. I am aware of my various roles in the history of the world back to Mesopotamia, the Tigris and Euphrates Valley. I won't bore you with the details, only to say that I am a Braided Soul who chooses to trade with my soul partner in the second half of the physical lifespan of the incarnation.

KM: And the death of the body?

WI: Death does not bother me. I think that birth is scarier. I leave that to my partner. But together we choose the mission/assignment carefully prior to the birth.

KM: So how does the Simultaneous Lifetimes work?

WI: All souls are Multi-dimensional and Limitless. We can transfigure or divide our integrated Self into smaller aspects to work on issues of a Karmic nature that have arisen during our previous missions. I am aware of three simultaneous existences at this time, but have only communicated with two of them. Ironically these three are the same gender as I am now. But if you believe in reincarnation and have experienced Past-Life Regression Therapy, you become aware of the fact that you have experienced all races, religions, and sexes.

KM: You mentioned Future Self?

WI: Yes. I am a Curandero in my next life. Although I should qualify that and say that that physical life has just commenced. The baby has been born. I generally rest for several years prior to assuming the next assignment, but we cannot afford the time off, if I can say that in a very American way. There is some urgency now.

KM: How would you define a Walk-In? Are all Walk-Ins Braided Souls?

WI: No, not all Walk-Ins are Braided. A Walk-In, I would say, is a soul personality who for one reason or another has taken on a mission in a human body by releasing another (with consent) from their mission in their human body. We are not intruders but crusaders of sorts, because without us the body would die anyway. The souls who evacuate the body have set the wheels in motion for the destruction of the body however they choose to do so. The Mind/Body connection should be Soul/Mind/Body connection, for that is the flow chart. If the Soul decides that it is weary or stunted in its growth, the Mind, then the Body get the message to abort the mission. The message is a death wish that actualizes. But a Braided Soul presets the Soul Exchange dates. There can be some overlap and flexibility though.

KM: So is there Someone, an "Overseer" perhaps who is in charge of this event?

WI: Of course. For our purposes we can call them Angels of Life or Light, but that is limiting the total understanding of their mission. They are Counselors. They transfer, carry, and deliver Energy for the Source of All Life.

KM: Can a Walk-In change their mind about walking in?

WI: Of course. We are discussing an opportunity for Spiritual Growth and Love.

KM: How is a Walk-In different from other people?

WI: Until we wake up, we tend to be confused, unhappy, and lost individuals. We are always beating ourselves up for not being like others, for not fitting into society's blueprint for success. For the most part we are never the cheerleaders or the jocks. Rarely are we fraternity or sorority members. We never fit into the elitist social structure no matter how hard we try or grieve to do so. And rarely do we bond well with our own bodies, so there is this phenomenon of internal discontent which keeps us at a certain level of constant agitation or aggravation. If we were talking about just the Body, it would be like allergies, skin problems or a rash, or a compromised immune system, but this is just at the Soul/Body level, so it gets even more intense sometimes when we consider the emotional impact of non-definition of self. Especially when you don't understand what the flap of life is all about, when you are young to it. Walk-Ins also possess certain anomalies or occult powers (although I dislike both words) that manifest in awareness as they gain experience, because they did not pass through the veil of birth. The sole reason for said powers (which are never merchandised or abused) is to better enable us to deliver our message to the world.

KM: What message?

WI: For humanity to get out of the terrible twos, the selfish twos, and look around. Every form of life on this planet is suffering because of our egocentric preoccupation with money and greed. What is money after all? It is all about controlling other people and raping the environment, raping Mother Earth. Our message is to wake up or there will be no future for us or any other form of life. On "Episode One" of Star Wars there is a scene of a planet where there is only city and masses of people. No other form of life exists on that planet. The entire planet is one big mass of concrete, steel, and humanity moving in a chaotic jam of traffic on and above the planet. Is that our vision for the future? I see it now, and it is not life, it is worse than death.

KM: What powers were you talking about?

WI: They don't really matter, except to those who would try to abuse them. To a Walk-In they are so second nature that they are taken for granted. I don't even like to talk about them, but the most useful to me has been clairsentience. Walking between worlds has also been most helpful to me on this journey. It is what brought me face to face with my Teacher.

KM: Who is your Teacher?

WI: I was told to call her "One Who Waits for the World." I call her Patience.

KM: And how does She teach you?

WI: What. She teaches love and compassion for all life. And much more of a personal nature that I'd rather not discuss.

KM: Are any of your siblings Walk-Ins?

WI: No. I believe it might be too much for a single family to cope with. (Laughs)

KM: Can one Walk-In identify another when they meet them?

WI: Instantly. After you are awake you know all kinds of things, and that is definitely one of them. You can sense and feel it.

KM: Do you know of Walk-Ins in history, like the history of the United States?

WI: When you read about their motivations you can pretty much tell. A Walk-In is not about personal or human aggrandizement, but the greater good of all life.

KM: Are there more Walk-Ins here now that were here, say at the birth of this nation?

WI: I have been told by my Teacher that there are more Walk-Ins here now than at any other time in history.

KM: And do you know why?

WI: Yes, and you do, too. The alarm clocks just don't seem to be loud enough to wake people up. Or maybe the holocaust sirens are making us all deaf or numb. We have reached a most critical time in history. The Tibetans call it the Kali Yuga.

KM: I have heard people refer to this as Atlantis all over again.

WI: But Atlantis was isolated, and there were expedient evacuations. This is global and there will be nowhere...nowhere to evacuate to. I am told that those in leadership are well aware of our collective destiny and have chosen to allow humanity to continue its present course in complacent slumber, yet throwing in a new car, a scandal, what they label a righteous war, or even inflation or a monetary crisis to keep us preoccupied.

KM: This all sounds pretty discouraging.

WI: I have heard you say countless times that there must be a change of consciousness for healing to occur. It is discouraging. Like moving boxes from one side of a building to another day after day, and then being told that it is the most important job that a person can have. We have to step away from all that and take a look at Truth. The Truth is discouraging, but we cannot change collectively until we look at it face to face and own what we have done. Each of us have done. There are no more "theys" to blame the state of our world upon. We must take responsibility for the health and well-being of our entire planet.

KM: While we mow, primp, and fertilize our little lawns, miles of rain forests are obliterated.

WI: And there is 20% less oxygen now than in the 1950's or 60's. We are creating our own dis-ease by disconnecting ourselves from nature, from Mother Earth Who heals us. We do not have the right to extinguish the life of other species to further our desires for more trinkets. And, if we expect machines or the mechanistic sciences to heal us, then we must first become machines or erroneously assume that we are already. Like the movie "Matrix." We will forget what life or living really is. We are in fact, becoming survivalists. You see it in the faces of adult Americans and far too many children who are hungry to be touched and nurtured.

KM: So, are you seeing, sensing, or predicting the end of the world?

WI: There are three probable outcomes that I have witnessed.

KM: Is it discouraging to you?

WI: At times. There is great joy and beauty in life as well, if you look for it. One of the outcomes is hopeful, spiritual in nature.

KM: So what is your best advice? Or should I say, what is your message?

WI: To continue, we need a planetary or cosmic goal. At this time in human history we lack what Star Trek calls a "Prime Directive." The Prime Directive honors all life, not just human life. Money is not the motivation, non-interference is. The message inherent in a global change of consciousness is far too threatening to the status quo. It is the tank and the student in Tiennamin Square. Change is too threatening to governments and power structures as it may cause death of the system. There is great fear of losing control over people and their money.

KM: So what will it take for change?

WI: Three generations taught deeper understanding. Generations who are raised in pure compassion and reverence for all life. These generations need teachers who are focused on the greater good or the global/cosmic perspective, what Carl Sagan calls "Deep Knowledge." A world built on love and trust, total equality, or even a common vision seems almost too good to be true. A world of Mahatmas...Great Souls like Gandhi. It is thwarting to disavow people on the grounds of sex or race.

KM: As a student of Thich Nhat Hanh's I would say that we should be studying the message from his book, <u>For a Future to be Possible</u>. We need to learn compassion for all life: in schools, on the job, in airports, everywhere.

WI: But instead we are forced into schools whose entire reason for being is to educate the masses to move those boxes from one side of the room to the other.

KM: So how does a Walk-In initiate a change in consciousness?

WI: By living a conscientious life. As Gandhi said, "My life is my example." And then allowing others to seek the same possibility for inner peace and right living in harmony with Mother Earth. Living the awakened life and then sharing the Path with others who are ready to walk on it with you.

KM: Is the Path wide enough for all of us?

WI: The Path is Unlimited. It transcends all time and all space. And when you find it you can only say to yourself, how could I have missed it all these years?

KM: But isn't it more difficult to live conscientiously?

WI: Of course it is. But as Walk-Ins, we see life as a broader perspective. We see the collective destiny of this planet whereas another human might have a difficult time moving beyond the daily grind of work-eat-TV-sleep. Then wake up when the alarm startles your eyes open and start all over again. I forgot to throw in a couple of Prozacs.

KM: So how would a Walk-In's life be different?

WI: Awareness makes all the difference, and it is possible for every person on Earth to become more aware. For example, our work would be our Path and it would honor us or we would not sell our souls or time on Earth for just money. In fact, we manifest such jobs for ourselves. We eat consciously. Most Walk-Ins are conscious eaters, attempting to honor all life is important. It also enables us to be healthier. We generally do not watch television nor do we get caught up in print drama, so we are useless for advertisers. I meditate so I do not find that I require as much sleep. But meditating is not just a Walk-In phenomenon. It prolongs life and health. I am aware of each and every breath that I breathe. But time is a living entity, so I am aware that it changes, evolves or devolves with us. So if people are caught on the wheel of survival, they need only to step off and look around at this wondrous world. If people believe that life is hard, then it will be. If they believe that they can be happy, then they make it happen. Life is a matter of perspective...instead of dreaming, we need to make the dream happen. Things happen twice; when we think them, and then when we make them happen.

Theater on Acropolis, Athens Greece
Photo by Matthew Mitchell

From: <u>*Mansions of the Soul, The Cosmic Connection*</u>
Written in 1930 by H. Spencer Lewis
"Two important principles are intimated by the symbolical or allegorical process of (humanity's) creation. First, that the physical body, made of the material elements of the earth, was completed and perfected as purely material before any consideration was given to the process of animating it with consciousness or life. Secondly, that with the physical body completed and yet lifeless, it was necessary for something more to be done to make it a living being, and that to do this there was added a second and distinctly different and separate element called 'the breath of life.' After this entered the physical body, the physical part became insignificant, for (humanity) was then not merely an animated body, or a physical body that was filled with life, but a <u>soul</u> that could live on earth and manifest itself and was, therefore, a <u>living soul</u>... We are impressed with the fact that the physical body did not take on life but that the invisible, infinite <u>soul</u> took on a physical form by the uniting of the breath with the body. Even the ancients were impressed with this significance and in their philosophies, which gradually evolved into theological principles, we are constantly reminded of the fact that humanity is essentially a <u>soul</u> clothed with a body, and not a body animated with a soul... The soul is, therefore only temporarily resident within a physical body and cannot remain eternally in one body, since in that case the body would have to be immortal, as is the soul... Therefore there comes a time when the physical body becomes disorganized and can no longer contain the soul. A change takes place which is incorrectly called death, but which is merely a transition. You are then face to face with the next important question: 'Why is the soul of God, or the Creator's consciousness, placed temporarily in a physical body, and what becomes of it after its release.

"That double question has been the most insistent and most important query in the consciousness of (humanity) since the dawn of thinking and believing."[1]

---

1. H. Spencer Lewis, Mansions of the soul, The cosmic Connection, The Rosicrucian Press LTD., San Jose California, 1930, pp. 44-46

Soul Braid
Twin Flame Braid

A "Soul Braid" is a soul connected in a single incarnational event to one other soul as a Twin Flame Braid. However, there are other possibilities that exist for a Braided Soul experience that can inherently consist of incarnational potential of one hundred and forty four combinations in a single lifetime. Generally the pattern is set for the braided switch to occur at various prearranged times in the life's journey of the individual. This process of Twin Flaming in one physical body is so embraced by some Walk-In souls that it is always their preferred context of incarnation. One member of the pair may enjoy being the child, the other may find childhood somewhat annoying and prefer the later stages of physical being. A Braided Soul combination may involve one or more pairs involved in the process of incarnation. One or more soul(s) may have very little Karma to work through in a physical form, so they "split" the obligation to the body. This may seem like the ultimate schizophrenia, but only one soul occupies the body for any length of time. The overlap occurs just prior to the exchange, and the other souls act, in the meantime, as Spirit Guides during the life's progression. In a Twin Flame Braid, the male aspect to the braid may choose to incarnate early on in the physical life of a female body. The male aspect may be working on early life or survival issues, or adjustment to the energy of the Earth Plane. It could also be that that aspect of the Twin Flame Soul enjoys the experience of youth as opposed to the rigidity or responsibilities of adult life. So the agreement is prearranged for that aspect of the twin to incarnate just prior to birth, at birth, or immediately following the physical birth of the body. During the womb-in bonding process, both souls commune with the physical body, moving in and out, nurturing, gaining knowledge and experience concerning the mother-father energies present. The First Aspect of the Twin Flame Soul spends more time in the last trimester bonding with the physical body and choosing and preparing its "jump site," where the soul will enter the physical body for retention for the duration of its stay. The Twin

Flame Transpirant remains attached to the other soul aspect even following the birth of the physical body. Depending upon the nature of the agreement, the other non-incarnated aspect may experience to some degree, the physical life that is occurring even though it is not "living" in the physical body. Memories are imprinted in the emotional body that both aspects co-own, so that no memories of value are lost in the transition or "Translation" process. When the Translation occurs, there is an easy transition from one soul force to another. The exchange is so subtle that rarely, if ever, is there any difference noticed by those related to the physical being. The exchange generally coincides with an age where there is an anticipated developmental change in the cultural adaptation. Generally this Translation process occurs best at seven or perhaps just preceding puberty. This accounts for the phenomenon of "gender phasing." In such cases, if the body is that of a female, and the male aspect of the Twin has entered first, the young female may display traits or be drawn to those activities more commonly aligned to the male attributes of a given culture. Then, suddenly, the little "tomboy" may (almost overnight) lose all interest in such activities and embrace the desired feminine qualities that the culture promotes. A butterfly miraculously emerges from the rough-edged cocoon of childhood. The opposite gender phasing may occur with the male body initiated into life with the female Twin. The transfer is completed sometimes, over the course of several weeks or months as the incoming Twin may "confer" with the body to adjust to the climate and confinement more gradually. During this time, subtle energy shifts are made with the electropositive, electronegative charge of the body to attract and hold the incoming vibration. It is as if the current is adjusted from an electrical current (in the case of the Male Twin) to the magnetic current phase (of the Female Twin). Actually, the two are in soul essence similar to the third dimensional concept of polar opposites, like magnets with North-South polarity, attracting each aspect of the Twin Flame essence. It is the Yin-Yang theory in practice. The dark half (the Yin) contains a seed of the light half (the Yang). The two halves are synergistic in nature, creating within the physical form a reaction with the soul's encounter with life-in-form.

The Twin Flame soul is what we would characterize as an ancient wanderer, seeking adventure and growth through actualizing in the physical form. Some believe that the Twin Flame or multi-braid soul is always a characteristic of a Pleiadian Soul, or a soul of the First Founding Energy such as an Essene. There are souls that were created from other sources, and souls of sorts (fragmented spirits) that were created by Atlantean technology. Such Earth bound spirits were created for specific working functions within the Atlantean, and later Egyptian cultures in the Central Complex of the Temple Beautiful. These spirits are still incarnating on the Earth Plane and are rarely concerned with soul growth. Their focus is rather upon three aspects of life: food, shelter, and sexual gratification. There is only a mechanical reference to a spiritual nature, as there is no inner core of being that can supply the depth of Love that is required for the generation of such true spiritual energy. They are drawn to religions that are mechanistic in nature, ones that help them to feel that they are fulfilling the cultural requirements for churching. These spirits are solitary, egocentric energies focused on the self and its needs. There are times that the Ancient Soul of the Twin Flame is attracted to such solitary soul individuals, but the attraction is generally at great cost physically, emotionally, and mentally for the Ancient Soul. The lesson comes from a desire of the ancient soul to "save" the solitary soul which the ancient soul views as merely stuck in the quagmire of life's lower meaning. They do not yet comprehend that the solitary soul is a "fixed soul," one that has no desire to advance toward enlightenment. Such ancient souls must learn the lesson of non-interference before they lose their attraction for saving solitary souls.

Merging of Twin Flame energy may occur in the body of an evolved individual during the course of a single lifetime. The individual evolves spiritually enough to acknowledge the presence of and communicate openly with the other aspect of their Twin Flame. The first awareness generates deep loneliness in the soul of the incarnate Twin. The incarnate Twin may enter into what has been called "the dark night of the soul," or feel a great suffering akin to grief or mourning. This expression of the awareness of loss-of-love is the awakening spiritually to the potentialities of Soul Merging. The incarnate Flame cries out continuously for the nurturing power of the other half. The soul dreams of the ideal spiritual marriage, of two compatible, pastel colors mingling and merging in the brilliant sunshine of another time. Eventually the hungry soul finds itself on the doorstep of those who assisted in the planning of this lifetime. A petition of Grace (through the Angel Charis) is presented to those primary Seven "Planners" of the Council of Sixty-four (referred to as the "Warden Angels" by some religious sects). It is reviewed instantly, and the Souls' desire for Mergence is generally granted. From that time on, the life of the Merged Twin Flames in physicality focuses most dramatically upon the pure Spiritual Nature of its existence. In the extreme, those related to them may feel that they have lost all sight of reality. The Merged Soul may relinquish all possessions and enter into a more spiritually fulfilling or monastic lifestyle. This is frightening to those relatives in the Western Cultures especially who still cling to material possessions as the summum bonum of life. On the contrary, the Merged Soul is quite content with poverty as long as the spiritual needs of the soul are met. This soul now cares very little for sex, the delights of food (and most generally embrace a vegetarian lifestyle), or indulge in extravagant comforts for the physical body. The Merged Soul has one purpose: to prepare to return to its Source, complete and whole, as it now is. There is a deep understanding that the life ongoing must be continued to its physical death, and obligations of the soul's commitments must be first fulfilled on the Earth Plane. A Merged Soul becomes a mystic and a mystery to those who know them, and they generally choose to live outside the cultural boundaries. True spiritual practice is easier on the fringes of community life, yet the soul is still able to assist others who are also seekers on the path to enlightenment. The Merged Twin Flame soul has a peace that transmutes all of the passion, all of the pain, and all of the melancholy of day-to-day existence. It is a life dedicated to Truth and Love.

Clans or Multi-Braids

There may be a sharing of soul energies similar to the Twin Flame phenomenon which involves two sets of Twin Flames up to combinations of seventy two such pairs (one hundred forty-four energies). These experiences are truly Divine Light in origin, and fulfill the need of the souls to assist in the spiritual development of others. Most often, this is a full-replacement experience where the original soul in the body may have been an Earth-created or solitary soul in distress.

The Twin Flame or Clan energies respond to the desperate pleas of the soul to vacate the physical body for one reason or another, and respond in assistance with a call to service. Such experiences are most often called into play in time of growth for the mother, the father, the society, the culture, or the planet. Miracles of healing can be attributed to such Divine Intervention, as the Guardian Angel or Divine Watcher may act as the replacement soul. In other cases, the function of "Stepping In" may be planned ahead of time for a soul who has very little karma to complete and is willing to step aside for another to take on the work at hand. Clans are often from the same soul source, such as we might call in a more limited sense "Soul-mates." The notion of compatibility of energy is taken into account. At times the calibration of vibratory force takes time, much like the experience of a body that might linger in a coma like sleeping beauty awaiting to waken once again to a world that is in waiting. The Translation process is a slower one when the body is not organically of a high frequency. A tuning process then occurs. Difficulties may arise later with the natal family, as the Walk-In never quite fits the established pattern of family life.

Ephesus, Turkey
Photo by Matthew Mitchell

The Canticle of Brother Sun by St. Francis of Assisi

...Praise be to Thee, my Lord, with all
    Thy creatures,
Especially Brother Sun,
Who is our day and lightens us
    therewith.
Beautiful is he and radiant with great
    splendor;
Of Thee, Most High, he bears expression.

Praise be to Thee, my Lord, for Sister
    Moon, and for the stars
In the heavens which Thou has formed
    Bright, precious, and fair.

Praise be to Thee, my Lord, for
    Brother Wind,
And for the air and the cloud of fair
    and all weather
Through which Thou givest sustenance
    to Thy creatures.

Praise be, my Lord for Sister Water.
Who is most useful, humble, precious and chaste.

Praise be, my Lord, for Brother Fire,
By whom Thou lightest up the night;
He is beautiful, merry, robust and strong.

Praise be, my Lord, for our Sister,
    Mother Earth,
Who sustains and governs us
And brings forth diverse fruits with
    many-hued flowers and grass.

The Contract

"I come to the Garden alone...while the dew is still on the roses..."

"But Francis, it's not time yet! I have five more years. I can't do this now."

"I am just presenting the facts to you. You do see that grave over there? If you do not go in soon, the body will perish. Die. It is the Law. Human bodies must have a soul to exist; it is more important than the brain, heart, or blood. I'm sorry that this happened. It was not part of the Master Plan for the two of you. He cannot go back. The cord is broken. It is up to you to fulfill the assignment, the contract, or let the child die. You have three of your Earth days to decide."

The little girl had been wandering for several hours in the orchard in the early morning hours before she realized that she had no physical body. She had imagined herself as she last remembered: red, plaid flannel shirt, knee-patched denim jeans, and "Red-Ball Jets" tennis shoes, small enough for a seven year old. Now she sensed a presence. There was someone there with her in the dew fresh grass of the orchard. He was silent at first, and then he spoke ever so softly to her. None of what he was saying made any sense to her, so she started to cry...crying with her spirit, since her warm body was a void, gone from its place around her.

"Am I dead?" she whispered?

The brown-robed figure responded, "No, no, not technically, not... exactly...you are...deciding, I believe." He said to her. Then he smiled with deep compassion.

"Who are you?" She was not afraid of him, rather in awe. She could not make out the facial features very well, but there was something very familiar about him. "No one else knows about this place. It's a secret."

"Oh, I've been here with you before, you just couldn't see me then. Now you can see me because...well, you're ready to. Tell me, what do you last remember?"

"Well, I was in the kitchen." She felt her image sink down deep in the dew-damp blue grass. "Mom was there, real worried. Dad didn't come home last night. Then, finally, the Chevy pulled in. She looked happy but scared. I think she thought he had left us all, the four of us. Dad was so drunk he couldn't open the door. She had to open the door and let him in. He thought she'd locked him out. He was really mad about that and throwing things off the table. Then he got worse when Mom was asking him questions about where he'd been and who he was with. He said he was at work and it was none of her business since she didn't work."

The little girl grew silent, thinking. "I lost the rest of it. I can't remember the rest of it." She started to cry again, drinking in deep gasps of spirit air between the sobs.

"Don't worry, it will come back to you when you're ready for it. Don't be afraid. Don't ever be afraid of anything my child."

* * * * * * * * *

It was thirty nine years later that the memory returned in regression therapy.

"All you have to do is allow your thoughts and emotions to flow easily and effortlessly. I want you to go back to the time that the

---

reason for your problem exists." "Abby" was spiraling down into a deep well of depression and decided to try Regression Therapy to find the root cause of the growing depression and more than occasional anxiety attacks. She nodded her head. "Good, are you there?"

She cleared her throat lightly. "I'm in what looks like a small, old kitchen. I see a tea-towel hanging on a clip of some kind. Oh, it's a clothes pin nailed by the sink. The floor is a dingy tile, off-white with specks in it. There is an old Frigidaire with rounded corners against the wall, across the kitchen there are six metal chairs with vinyl seats and table with a yellowish top. The ashtray is on the counter is full of cigarette butts. I smell burned coffee."

I leaned forward to hear better, as Abby's voice trailed off softly at the end of each sentence. I continued. "Are you alone or with someone?"

"Mom. She's leaning against the sink, drinking coffee, smoking a cigarette. She looks really young. I don't ever remember her looking so young. She's wearing a print cotton dress. She's upset about something; chewing her lip and looking out the window every few minutes. The dog's here too. I'm petting the dog. He's young and jumps around a lot. He licks me in the face and I laugh. Mom tells me to go into the other room. I'm in the way in the kitchen." Abby falls into silence, and her eyes flutter beneath the lids as if scanning the room for more information. "I know where this place is." She grew breathless. "I never liked it there. The house was too small for us and we never had a bed to sleep in. We all slept on the couch except for Mom and Dad. They had their own room, but you could still hear them fighting all the time in there."

"Where are you, Abby? Where is this place located?"

"The place is in the country where we went after they took us away."

"Took you away? Who took you away?" There was no answer. "Away from what Abby?"

"My aunt and grandma. They really loved us." She started to cry. "They protected us from him. My aunt raised me from the time I was a baby. But he was always there drinking and yelling and hurting everyone."

"Who took you away?"

"Dad did, when my Aunt... did something he didn't like."

"Did you want to go?"

"No. I thought I could stop him. I wanted to stop him! I wanted to kick and scream and hurt him so he'd leave me alone. But I was too scared. That's why I wouldn't eat. That really made him mad. I didn't want to be there, with them. I wanted my aunt and my grandma. Mom and Dad didn't care about me, about us. We were just in the middle of it all. I wanted to die."

"So, Abby, you stopped eating?" I made a note, thinking that this may have been the root cause of the depression.

"Yes. First they tried to fix my favorite food. Then he tried to force me to eat with his fist. Mom would cry and he'd hit her. Then he started to get really mean to me about it."

"What do you mean, 'mean about it'?"

"He would yell, jerk me off my chair, hit around on me, pry my mouth open and stuff food in, that sort of mean thing. He hurt a tooth and it bled." I considered the next question carefully. "So, what happened next?"

"I hid out a lot to keep away from him. I hid in the orchard.

There's a secret place I go to to hide. No one knows where it is. I can hear them yelling at me, but I won't come out."

"Are you there now?"

"No. I just woke up. It's real early, almost still dark outside. No one is ever up then. I like to leave before they get up."

"To go to school?"

"No, it's summer. No school. I need to get to the orchard before they see me. Oh no, Mom's there. In the kitchen. I know she won't let me out until I do some chores for her." Silence follows.

"Abby, go on." I suggest.

"She almost doesn't see me. Then she does. She asks me why I'm up so early, but she doesn't really care about an answer. It's like I'm there to her but not really. She tells me that Dad didn't come home last night. She's talking and talking and then she is crying. The dog is jumping around, wanting to go out with me. I feel stuck there, like I don't know what to feel or do. She says we'll starve if he doesn't come back. I don't care. I don't want him to come back...ever."

"And what happens next?"

"The car pulls in loud and fast, and too close to the house, right by the door. Dad falls out of the car. Mom opens the door. He's kicking on it. He falls in the door. He's throwing stuff. Mom asks him where he's been all night. He yells real loud about it being all her fault for everything. For him working so hard. The dog jumps up on him, happy he's home. He kicks the dog really hard in the head. I'm screaming for the dog, but he's not moving. He yells to me to shut up and hits me hard on the face. Mom gets scared...she grabs a knife. She won't do anything. I know she won't. So does he. So she drops it. He laughs at her. He kicks her hard in the legs, then punches her in the stomach. *No more brats in this house, do you understand?* I grab his arm to stop his hitting her. He throws me against the corner of the wall. I taste blood in my mouth, my head is spinning, and then there's a buzzing sound. Then there are morning birds singing louder than I've ever noticed. I'm in the orchard now."

I am a bit lost. I then ask, "How did you get there?" But I think I know.

"I think I ran out of the house, maybe. I don't remember how I got there. I just remember being there. That's where I wanted to go, I guess."

After a few moments, I continued. "So tell me, what happens next?"

"Francis is there, talking to me. Trying to get me to go back."

"Who is Francis?"

"The man in the brown dress and rope belt. He loves animals as much as I do." Her voice is like a young girl's voice. "I tell him I don't want to go back. Then I see my dog. My dog is running up to me. But he runs right through me. Like I'm not even there. How did he do that? My dog! Where is my dog going?"

Francis touches my arm. He's going on now. He won't be back you know. He can't come back. He doesn't have a choice to make like you do. The choice has been made for him."

"You mean...my dog is dead? He killed him?"

"Yes, child, Abby, I am afraid that is true." Then Francis shows me a piece of ground with a big rock on it, hiding the dug up dirt. There's no grass on the ground there. Just dirt and the rock, under the canopy of a white cherry tree. "I know what it is!" Abby seems startled and anxious. Her breathing is irregular and labored. "My grave! It's...my grave! They...he...will bury me there like my bird, and not tell anyone about it. Like I never was born in the first place." Abby starts to cry, still struggling for every breath.

I recognize her breathing as an abreaction, the release of emotionally charged material from the subconscious mind into the conscious mind. "Go just beyond this, to the other side of this, Abby. Breathe easily and effortlessly. Breathe in peace now, and relax. Good. Just relax for a few moments. Breathe in peace and breathe out light."

She takes a deep breath and once again grows still and silent. She is breathing evenly now. "Nothing's happening. I'm in school now, and my teacher is upset that I can't learn to put the right numbers in the clock. It's one of those puzzles, a plastic clock where only the right number peg will fit into the slot by the hour. The teacher tells me how dumb I am, and wants me to stay in from every recess to do the clock thing. She turns out the lights leaves me there alone in the classroom with the lights out. I don't mind the alone, but I hate being inside. My desk is by the corner. I fall asleep a lot during school but I don't know why. My teacher just lets me sleep. She likes it quiet."

"Abby, what grade is this?"

"Second I think. Yes, second grade. My mind is different than it was before and is now. I don't see things right. The colors are faded, and I spin in my head sometimes. I don't always understand words or hear directions right. I get confused and go backwards." Then suddenly she cries out, "It's like I'm mentally retarded or something. It's not me! This isn't me. It can't be me!" Her voice changes to a woman's voice once again. "She's dyslexic...the child is dyslexic. But that is not me, it can't be me. I don't even remember any of this."

"Who is it then Abby?"

She is quiet for several minutes. "I wouldn't go back." She starts to cry again. It is the girl's voice again. "He says he'll hold the space for awhile longer, until I decide for certain. I'm just sitting there in the corner; too weak and too... vulnerable."

"Who is the one you keep calling 'he'? I was confused.

"Francis. He's waiting for me to decide. Holding the place like a bookmark. He's acting like a Marker for me."

"What do you mean, 'Marker'?"

"A Marker Soul. A soul who helps to keep the body alive, until the decision to live, die, or an exchange is made."

I am not completely certain that I understand what Abby has said. "So how long does Francis stay there, to keep the body alive for you?"

"I'm not sure. It was never long enough. I feel that in my heart. I needed more time. I was supposed to have five years before I had to go in. That was the contract."

Glancing at the clock, I knew that it was time to complete the session for this week. It had been about sixty-five minutes. Slowly, I counted Abby out of the regression session.

"I think my feet are asleep."

"Move them around a little bit, Abby, and they'll be all right. You were under for more than an hour. That sometimes happens in longer regression sessions. How do you feel about your experience?"

She sighed heavily and sat up in her chair. "A big part of me doubts that it happened. I just don't remember any of that. I was told that I did have an imaginary friend, though. My sisters used to tease me about it and my mom and dad told me to stop talking about him in front of other people. My grandmother used to set a place at the table for him." She laughed. "She talked to him too, but I think it was just to humor me. It made my parents furious." Chewing her lip she reflected. "It reminds me of Don Juan. Have you ever read any books by Carlos Castaneda?"

"No, I don't think so."

"Well, he has many...experiences that he tries to explain. But it is difficult sometimes. One time there was a strange gust of what he calls wind. But then Don Juan says to him, 'It may seem like wind to you, because wind is all you know'."

I thought for a moment. "So you don't remember any of this, of your...experience before our regression?"

"Places...the house...the school building...the car. But I completely forgot the dog. But now I remember him and it makes me really sad." She tried to bite back the tears. "You know, I was really sick. I was out of it for days. Just now I remember what they told me the dog..." she took a deep breath to continue. "They told me that the dog was hit by a car and died. Dad buried him. He was black and white. Short sleek hair and perky ears." Her eyes were welling up.

"Why were you so sick?"

"I don't remember." The tears trickled down the sides of her cheeks.

"Did they take you to see a doctor Abby? When you were so sick?"

"No." Her voice was a faint echo.

"Don't you suppose that a child that sick would or should see a doctor?"

"Oh no," she laughed quietly. "You don't know how it was in that house. No one went to the doctor. You were never really sick...only faking it to get out of something you didn't want to do. Which I never did. I always wanted out of that house, no matter how sick I was. Or what chores I had to do. It was the opposite."

I moved forward in my chair. "Did anything change after that... that you remember?"

"You know, now that I think about it. We started seeing my aunt and grandma again. Not a lot, just now and then. But he said we would never see them again because of the fight they had with them. He was nasty to them. And then we moved back to the same town a year later. I started a new school. I loved my third grade teacher. She was so... nurturing. After we moved away from there I felt a lot different. I just felt lost before...Wow, there are some things that are starting to make sense to me now. All of that missing time."

"Next week when you come in we'll see if we can put this whole thing together in your mind so you can start to feel better."

"It's funny, but I do think I feel better already. And I want to thank you for that."

"You do all the work," I replied. "I just listen."

As Abby walked out into the September sunshine, I know that she must have felt a deep sense of peace. It was as if her life, her existence had been broken down into two parts, like a before chapter and an after chapter. I was sure she wanted to know more of the truth about the before chapter.

The week passed quickly for Abby, and soon she returned to my office. It was raining, and her spirits seemed to be dampened by the rain.

I greeted her at the door. "How have you been Abby? Come on in and tell me how your week has been."

"It seems that when I'm not busy doing something, an old memory comes in. It's like I'm being haunted by a past I don't remember, but now it's remembering me." She smiled.

"Any anxiety attacks this week?"

"No, now that you mentioned it. I never even thought about it."

"Good." I opened the door to my inner therapy office. "How about dreams? Any of those?"

"It's interesting that you ask me that." Her eyes grew big. "Yes. I kept dreaming the same dream. Like someone trying to tell you something and you're not quite getting it. Do you know what I mean?"

I motioned for her to sit down. "Can I get you some water?"

"No, no thanks." She continued. "I keep seeing a monastery in my mind. I can even hear monks talking and singing. Not like that Chant song, but old holy songs of some sort. In Latin. Then one of them comes up to me, one of the monks. I'm just a little shabby, snot-nosed kid hiding in the corner. At first I don't recognize myself. But then I notice the tennis shoes and the shirt. The monk says something to me and puts out his hand. I know that he is talking to me, but I can never remember. I had that dream a couple of times. When I wake up my pillow is wet."

"You were crying?" I asked.

"It would seem so, but I don't remember that either. Can you cry in your sleep and not know you were crying?"

"You might be chelating out some deep emotions that we have uncovered in our session before," I said, reflecting, taking a quick note, but trying to keep my eyes on Abby.

"Maybe." Her voice was skeptical. "But I do think there's more to it than that. Could this be a past life thing?"

"It could be, but the key might be the type of clothes you saw that child wearing in the dream." I replied.

"Yeah, it was that same red plaid shirt...faded, patched blue jeans...red high-top tennis shoes with ragged laces. Funny the details you remember in a dream. Oh, the monk's hand. I nearly forgot!" She looked a bit excited. "The same monk in my regression was in the dream. Francis. But the hand that he held out had thick blood running down from his palm to his middle finger."

"The stigmata?"

"The what?" Abby asked.

"You aren't Catholic then?"

"No, no I'm not. Methodist. Why?"

I looked at Abby, wondering if I should have mentioned it. It knew it might somehow be leading, or revealing something she should learn herself. "Oh, well...nothing, really." I looked down at my notes.

"I already have an idea that I thought of. At first I thought that the monk might be Jesus, but I knew that that wasn't true. He was the same Francis. I think he was St. Francis. The one who loved animals. But maybe he had been crucified like Jesus. Was he? Is that what this 'stigmata' means? If you don't want to tell me, I'll just have to go look it up. If I'm right you can tell me, no, no, never mind, I'll just look it up. My assignment." She gave me a knowing smile as if she understood what I was thinking.

"Shall we begin our regression session?" I smiled back at her, standing. "Where would you like to begin today? Should we take a deeper look at your dream, or shall we pick up where we left off last time?"

I felt that she was not really listening, but rather reflecting on some other topic. "You know what is funny Dr. Mitchell? I memorized the Serenity Prayer of St. Francis when I was eight. I'm not certain it is really his though. I've never forgotten it: 'Lord, Make me an instrument of Thy peace. Where there is hatred, let me sow love...where there is injury, pardon'..." she stopped. "Well, you've heard it." I nodded. Then she continued, "My favorite was the last part, 'Oh Divine Master, grant that I may not so much seek to be consoled as to console, to be understood as to understand. To be loved as to love.' It still brings tears to my eyes. I think I memorized it because it helped when my parents were fighting all the time...I imagined that I was the peacemaker. How I tried. I still hate for people to disagree or fight. I used to throw myself in the middle." She paused. "Not a good place to be...in the middle of a fight that has no beginning or no end. Nietzsche said, 'When you look into the abyss, the abyss looks into you.' Their fights were like a great black hole."

"So you tried to bring peace like all of us good little co-dependent children do?" I smiled. Remember our very first discussion... about Melody Beattie's book, <u>Co-Dependent No More</u>...?

"Of course I do. I'm certainly not endorsing the role that I played in the family. Nor do I recommend it to anyone. Well, if I may choose where to start, I guess we might begin where we left off, maybe. I have to tell you this, though. I didn't want to come today. I really fought it. I think I'm afraid of what else I might find out. Things that I've stuffed away so I don't have to look at them. The truth is, I'm pretty good at talking around or hiding my feelings. But I've decided to be as painfully honest with you and with myself as I can bear to be. Tears welled up in her eyes. "Who would want to know this old painful stuff? Is it relevant anymore? I feel lighter when I leave, but I certainly don't look forward to the excavation. It's like dental work. You don't want to go. In fact, I've heard that dentists have the highest no-show and cancellation rate of any doctors." She reached for a tissue in her purse. Blowing her nose she said, "See, there I go with the nervous chatter. I do the same thing at the dentist office. We just all want to remember the good times when we were growing up, like the Nelsons on "Ozzie and Harriet" or "Leave It To Beaver"...not the constant fights or the pain, or the drinking."

"I know how you must feel. It is hard to imagine why or how someone would hurt someone else. But you also have to understand how alcohol...how your parent's drinking, affected them. If we understand the pain of where we've been it makes our present moment so much more powerful, more meaningful. Like facing our fears and our demons head on."

"Oh, I know that pretty well. Demons and fears. Fighting and forgetting the next day, so surreal. All my life with both of them drinking and fighting. It was like living with Dr. Jekyll and Mrs. Hyde. They would say and do awful things when they were drunk, and the next morning it was like nothing ever happened. To them, I was an ungrateful troll at night, and a lovely untouchable princess in the morning."

"The elephant in the living room story."

"I'm afraid I don't know that one."

"It goes like this...in dysfunctional homes, especially where there is alcohol involved, everyone knows there is an elephant in the living room. Everyone in the family sees it but no one can talk about it, especially to guests or people outside of the home. So the elephant just sits there in the living room, taking up so much space, and everyone tries to go about their life as if it really wasn't there."

Abby laughed. "But I think we had a herd of elephants. There were always things we weren't supposed to tell anyone, ever, or else! I always wondered what that 'or else' was. But I think I always knew the implication. It was just like with grades or actions. 'Be perfect, or else!' Or else... they wouldn't love you. It was the worse case scenario. But the irony of it was, the love wasn't really there to begin with. Instead of love it was always, to me at least, 'what can you do for me.' Conditional love, I think they call it. The elephants were definitely there."

"Sometimes I wonder if no love is better than conditional love. Conditional love in the childhood certainly keeps us counselors busy enough. Are you ready Abby?"

"I think so," she sighed.

"Good. then just relax and close you eyes..."

Abby spoke in incomplete run-on sentences, descriptions. She said that she was back in the orchard. The sun was setting in the sky just beyond the trees. She could see the orange of the sky emerging through the trunks of assorted fruit trees. She knew that the family would be eating dinner soon. She wondered about the body, her body. Was it really dying? At that moment of thought, she was there, standing beside the brown couch in the tiny living room. People, noises echoed around her, fading in and out. They were there but not really there. then she saw the small body stretched out on the couch. Shoes off now. A towel on the side of her head. Dripping ice melting down her neck. So small. Fragile, and insignificant. Alone. Very alone. Waves of intense pain, like the concentric circles of a stone dropped into still water, waved through her awareness. Her head and her heart ached. She held her hand up to her head and started to sob silently. "It hurts. It hurts to cry."

"Abby. Abby." I called out to her.

"Voices seem like ripples through thick water. There's something wrong with my head... or with my ears. I don't know! I can't hear things that make sense. I'm afraid. My head is full and spinning. Alone. I think I'm dying. Maybe I'm dead already." She moans and cries and holds her head.

I directed her back to consciousness. I told her that she could hear me clearly now, that she was back in this room at this time, remembering everything.

She sat up abruptly. "The room is still spinning. I feel...nauseous."

"You are here Abby. Feeling better and better. Your feet are on the floor, You are here in my office. Safe, warm, and protected. Remember?"

Her eyes were vacant, withdrawn. "What happened to me?"

"I'm not sure. The room is still spinning and my head aches horrible. It's throbbing."

"Put your finger below your nose and press firmly." I demonstrated. "Now take three deep breaths and focus on one thing in the room." She focused on a fuzzy bear on the desk.

"What is the bear for anyway?" Abby asked.

"Simon helps children and inner children to heal." I smiled at her. "Better?"

"Yes, the room is not spinning, but my head still aches. Funny, I remember my grandpa used to have me chew on small willow sticks or bark for headaches. I had a lot of them when I was a kid. And earaches." Then it dawned on her why she had those headaches. "No wonder I had headaches." She muttered aloud. "I saw her...me...on the couch...they had put some ice in a dishtowel on her head. I really think she was dying. And they just left her there and were eating in the kitchen like nothing had happened. That was the pain I felt. The pain in my head."

"We still have forty minutes or so. Do you want to go back there?" I asked. "I think it might help you to get some resolution once and for all."

"I don't really want to go back there. I'm afraid of the pain. Can we go to the monastery place, the place in my dream, instead?"

"If that's what you want. Are you sure you are up to it?"

"I don't want to waste your time, and besides, I'm curious."

"You have to cancel that time-wasting idea. Remember the positive self esteem and all that healing work with Louise Hay?"

"Okay. I get the point." She leaned back in the recliner. She said it felt soft like a cloud around and under her. I counted slowly from ten down to one. Abby said that she felt herself sinking deep down into the fabric of the chair. Then she said she heard a muffled voice in her head.

"Where are you?"

"I am looking up directly into the smiling face of that monk. "Oh!" she said. I watched her expression change from surprise, to sadness, to an impish look of joy.

"He wants me to come with him. To meet someone. He is holding out a bleeding palm to me. He is reading my thoughts. I don't want to touch him. I don't like blood. He says, 'Don't worry about the blood, it purifies the soul.' He is smiling and asking me to trust him. He says, 'Trust me. I would never harm you.'

His smile is soothing. I look up at him from the corner where I am sitting...in the monastery. The stone blocks are cold and gray. Francis makes up for it with his warm touch. He lifts me from the floor. I am tiny, small."

'Meet who?' I ask him. I hope it is my dog.

'A boy.' He wants me to meet a boy. He says I know this boy.

We walk down a dingy hallway and into a small room with by a crucifix on the wall. A young boy is huddled in a fetal position on a makeshift straw mattress. He tells me the boy's name is Benjamin. The boy is apologizing to me for leaving. I don't know what he is talking about. He says the blow to the head was too hard, and where it hit broke something. I think he said the rope broke and he had to leave."

"Abby, what happens next..." I ask.

"Francis is talking. Something about the Law of Souls and our contract." *She is quiet for about five minutes. I sensed that there was dialogue going on,. and did not want to interrupt. Then she said, "You know, my head is starting to hurt again. I really feel sorry for this boy here, but this is too confusing. It doesn't make sense. Why would I always want to come in later? What agreement?" She was confused and started to cry. "No, I don't know. I don't know, I don't remember!"*

"Abby. Abby! I'm going to count from one to three and you will be just beyond this and back in this room at this time, remembering everything. One, two, and three!" I snapped my fingers.

Abby's eyes blinked and then opened wide. She realized that she had been crying, and wiped her cheeks and eyes with the tissues that I handed to her. Her mind was once again blank. "What happened?" she asked.

"You don't remember talking to Francis and Benjamin?"

"No, I guess not. My brain feels like I'm in a deep fog. A sleepy hangover."

I pushed the rewind button on the tape recorder. "Would you like to take the tape home and listen to it Abby?"

"Should I?" She sat up, holding her face in her hands, exhausted.

"That's up to you entirely. I gave you a suggestion to 'remember everything,' but your mental processes may still be protecting you, blocking a bit."

"Protecting me from what?" Abby's voice was quiet and uncertain.

I was careful with my response. "The Truth as you define it."

"Truth?" Abby's mind was back on track. She said that it flipped first from Mohandas Gandhi and then to "The Outer Limits" television program. She started to laugh sarcastically. When she was stressed her mind offered such humorous contrasts. "Truth. Gandhi said in his autobiography "<u>Experiments with Truth</u>" that 'There is no other God than Truth...that self realization is equated with Absolute Truth, like seeing God face to Face.' This makes me think of an episode of

---

"The Outer Limits". It was about genocide of an alien race on a foreign planet for human colonization. The karmic twist is that the humans all end up dead because they refuse to listen to the truth about their hostile planet. The moral sticks with me...'Humanity goes to great lengths to discover the truth only then to choose to ignore it.'" She laughed aloud again, inspired by the irony. "So what should I do? What would you do?" She brushed her hair back off her forehead.

"I would listen to this tape when and if you're ready. If you listen to it, we can talk about your thoughts when you come back next week."

"Okay." She gathered her bag and jacket. "Maybe I should rent that old movie 'Brother Sun and Sister Moon.'" She saw my blank expression. "It's about St. Francis of Assisi and Clare Scifi...St. Clare...Brother Sun and Sister Moon. 'Brother Sun who is our day and lightens us; Sister Moon for the stars in the Heavens which Thou has formed bright, precious and fair...'"

"Sounds more like Shakespeare," I smiled at her.

"Does it? 'Life is but a walking shadow... a poor player who struts and frets its hour upon the stage and then is heard no more.'"

"'Filled with sound and fury, signifying nothing'...it really makes you wonder what he would have written if he...Shakespeare...was put on Prozac."

"Or Ritalin as a child." She smiled as she left, looking now much lighter, almost elated. I knew that her life was somehow changing.

It was two weeks before I saw Abby again.

She was smiling. "I did my research," she said. I looked at her, not certain I understood. "On the Stigmata. Interesting. I wasn't far off with what I thought it was. The Stigmata is a...phenomenon, a religious event, where blood comes from the hands, feet, and one side of the body. It mimics the wounds of Christ. The most recent person to have the Stigmata was a priest named Padre Pio. It was a considered a miraculous sign of holiness. It was believed that if a person touched the Stigmata blood or wound, it was supposed to immediately heal disease. It mimics the wounds of Christ after the crucifixion. It was the cause of St. Francis' death. He received the Stigmata from a visit by an angel with six wings. They say that he, St. Francis, did too much for others; he...allowed others to touch the stigmata wounds in his hands so much that it caused a massive infection in his body. His followers begged him to stop, to rest and heal himself for awhile, but he would not. He couldn't turn away anyone who was suffering... he just had too much compassion for others. So he died after living in constant pain for over two years. They say he suffered from a massive infection throughout his entire body. Before he died he added a final stanza to his canticle "Brother Sun and Sister Moon:"

"Praised be our Lord for our sister, the bodily death,
From which no living man can flee,
Woe to them who die in mortal sin,
Blessed those who shall find themselves in Thy most holy will,
For the second death shall do them no ill."

"The second death?" I asked, "What do you think that means?"

"I'm not certain, but I was caught up in the fact that he calls death a 'sister'." She smiled at me. "I think death is more Yang than Yin."

I changed the subject. "Did you get a chance to listen to the tape?"

She handed it back to me. "Yes. It was..." she hesitated. "It didn't make much sense to me. Did you know what was going on when we were in the session?"

"I have thought about it, but I've learned not to try to interpret things. Would you like some tea or water?" I asked.

"Spice would be nice, if it's decaffeinated."

I handed the cup of tea to her. "Have you had anymore dreams?"

"Just about my father. He wanted my help, but when I tried to help him he told me to stop. I used to dream about houses with water running through them all of the time. Some fantastic mansions, and others more woodsy. I also dream about strangers; their lives and events that I knew were happening now, but I didn't have a clue. It was like I was a part of a family and I didn't recognize anyone, but they all knew and recognized me."

"Did you recognize you? Were you able to see yourself there?" I asked.

"Yes, but I never look like me." She sipped her tea. "Like the last dream I had months ago. I was on a ferry boat, bringing my horse back from Nantucket to Wood's Hole. It was all very real. I knew exactly where I was and what was going on, even though I had just entered the dream. I had all senses, and I was shocked that I could see much more clearly. I remember thinking to myself that my eyes were better than they are. I had long brown hair, brown eyes, and was very aware that I was rich." She laughed. "There was a Jaguar car involved somewhere. The family of unknowns lived in an estate in Falmouth. My father was with me, and we were bringing the horse to the mainland for some sort of competition, a 'cup event' of some sort. I think the girl was spoiled and pretentious." She laughed again. She seemed to be in a very good humor today. "Not like me at all."

"Where did the dream end for you?" I asked.

"That's the funny part. I'm not sure it did. I don't remember anything stopping or ending, like a television show might end, or a novel. It was as if everything was going on, like I'd stopped for...tea," she held up her cup, "and then just phased out of the scene. I do remember talking to my father, the I don't know who you are father, and his voice just kept getting more faint until I couldn't hear it anymore."

"So, what do you suppose it means?" I asked.

She smiled. "Maybe that I am burning the candle at both ends. I never have slept well at night. Maybe I have a secret life when I'm asleep here, and vice-versa."

"It sounds exciting but a bit stressful to me." I glanced at the clock. "I think we should get started on today's session, if you're ready."

"I'd like to find out more about my childhood bout with the dyslexia if that is all right with you?" She stretched back in the recliner.

I gave Abby the suggestion that she would go back to the time of the reason for her dyslexia. There was a long silence and then:

"I'm in the kitchen again...where the fight took place. Now I am lying on the couch with the melting ice on my head...bleeding and pounding. I feel like I must sleep a lot, and when I wake up there is so much pain and dizziness. The room spins." She is suddenly

silent.

"Abby...how long did you... sleep?" I asked.

Her answer was strange. "In the body or out?" Her voice had changed.

"Please explain your answer if you would," I said.

"The body was in a coma for over four days. I came in for three and decided I could not handle the pain and I was not certain I wanted to complete this particular life assignment. We do have ultimate choice you know. I know you know that. We all do know that on some level. I knew that the situation might get worse. This was an event that we had not..." she hesitated. "We had not planned."

"Who had not planned, Abby?" I knew I was now communicating with Abby's Higher Self.

"Benjamin and I...and others. But we have done this since we first arrived. Sometimes it is easy, sometimes not so easy. The assignment is what is important, what comes first in consideration. In this case, it was mostly Benjamin who thought we should consider the extenuating circumstances and undertake this particular assignment." She was suddenly quiet.

I wanted to go on, I wanted to know more. "Abby, What were the extenuating circumstances?" I asked gently.

"There were two from our soul group...this gets complicated. Two who were braided like us decided to incarnate in separate bodies and be together. One gave birth to the other in fact. It was an evolved, yet risky event in our particular soul stream. Something there did not go quite as planned and Benjamin saw an opportunity to join them and assist with their mission." Silence again, as if Abby, deep in thought, was listening. We do try to assist all life, in fact. That is the primary focus of our soul group.

"Is St. Francis a member of your group?" I ask.

"Yes and no. It would be better to say that we are members of his group, as our focus is shared...to assist all life, but he is not really attached to our particular group."

"He has his own group?" I wondered.

"He does not have a Braided Soul Source. He was before. He is what we call a Primary." It was as if she was reading my thoughts. "A Primary is not better or more advanced, it is just different. The way an architect is not a construction worker but both work on building. And both are needed to create the building structure."

"So you and Benjamin are Braided?"

"Yes," she replied after a long pause. "He was supposed to remain in the body longer. It was our agreement, our contract. But the chord was severed in the..." Abby struggled for the right word. "When there was the blow to the side of the head. I was called in. He could not go back. I was already attached, but the pain was almost too much to bear. I was not used to coming in with extreme pain. But many who walk in do come in and revitalize and restore a dying body to bring forth a commitment or a message to the world of humanity. The Angel St. Michael merged, entered the body, to complete the message for the suffering St. Francis. That is why he came to us...to me. He understood the pain and wanted to carry it for me." She moved her hand to her heart. I noticed tears welling in her eyes.

"How did he do that?" I asked her.

"He was...is a Primary. He could interface with almost any body. He held the space, he was the Marker for me until I decided to completely enter the assignment." The tears now rolled down her cheeks.

"How long did he...stay in the space?" I wanted to word the question correctly.

"For over a year. But time was not so much what mattered, it was the energy of the body that eventually deteriorates and then it becomes diseased. It takes a toll on the body."

"Was that the dyslexia?" I asked. "The brain was deteriorating?"

"It was more like autism. The brain was fading out like a dimmed light. I watched all this. I know that Francis did not mind doing this, none of us would mind...but I have never in my incarnations been faced with...well with the life ahead."

"Were you afraid that she would be mentally retarded Abby?"

"No. that wasn't it. There was more to it than just that. It was the next step in our particular evolution, and I was surprised that it had come to us so soon. But in my heart, I knew that this was a gift, that it was time."

I was aware that our time was growing short. I asked, "Is there anything else that needs to be healed here?"

She spoke in a slow, clear voice: "'Voce mea ad Dominum clamavi: voce mea ad Dominum deprecatus sum. Effundo in conspectu ejus orationem meam: et tribulationem meam ante ipsum pronuntio.' Peace. I am ready for peace. I cannot change the past, so ask for help to transcend it. Receive my prayer for peace. Make me an instrument of Thy peace. Allow me to bring peace into my own life too."

I later asked Abby if she was speaking in Latin. She was not aware that she was speaking a foreign language at all, and did not know Latin.

In our final session, Abby seemed to be quite different. She was confident that her depression was completely gone. She had had a dream which explained, she felt, the reason for her bouts with extreme depression during the last year:

"I was in a hospital that had maybe sixteen or twenty beds...small metal-type beds lined up on two walls of a long room. The beds were sticking out to the middle of the room with maybe three feet between each bed. The paint in the room was a dingy white. In places the ceiling paint was peeling off. This was not an American Hospital, and at first I thought that I might be having a past-life experience. I walked to the bed of an old woman. A woman from India. She was curled up in pain, in a fetal position, dying a slow death. She looked up at me as if she recognized me. She said that she had been calling for me. I asked her if she knew who I was. She said that she did; she called me by the name that my grandmother used to call me. I asked her why she had been calling me. She said that she was also me, and that she did not want to die alone. And she knew that I would come. I spent some time with her, brushing her long hair, soothing her any way that I could. Sitting with her. Listening to her breathe as she slept. There was very little verbal dialogue until the end. It occurred to me that I didn't even speak her language. A day or two later, she woke up and thanked me for coming. She said that while she was a part of me, we lived different vedic soul aspects in separate life forms (she actually used the word 'container' instead of 'form'.) She apologized for making me so sad in her dying process, as that was not her intention. I asked the Universe for a blessing for her for a harmonious exit and a more elevated spiritual rebirth, if there was to be one. I felt like I was losing my mother. When I woke up the next morning I knew that she had died. I remember witnessing her soul leaving her body like a soft cloud. At that moment I felt both happy and sad. She was free! I suddenly felt much lighter in my spirit. Like a heaviness or dark cloud had been lifted. Even taking a breath seemed more peaceful. I know that this work has helped me more than I will ever know. Even if what happened was not what we expected. Even if what happened was just a dream..."

"Abby," I said, "You asked for peace, and it came to you. Just not the way you had planned. When we give up our need to control life or events, they become easier to heal. Like the saying, 'Let go and let God...'"

"So, you think the hospital dream may have been real? Do you believe in simultaneous lifetimes or co-existence?" She asked.

I knew that I did, but did not know exactly how to express my awareness to her. "If you are asking me if co-existence is possible, I can only say that I believe that anything is possible. Einstein once said that 'common sense is that layer of prejudices laid down in the mind prior to the age of eighteen.'" We were both silent for a few moments and then I shared with her another quote, this one from the poet Kahlil Gibran: "'Trust in the dreams, for in them lies the gates to eternity.' Even if I didn't think that your dream or experience was 'real,' it doesn't matter. What matters is that your depression is gone."

She smiled, also thinking of a quote. "Who was it that said, 'We are such things as dreams are made of?'"

> *"The distinction between the past, present, and future is only an illusion, even if a stubborn one."* Albert Einstein

**Cathedral
at Bath**
Photo by Shauna
Angel Blue

Marker Soul

*"All those who lived in the past
live in us now. Surely none of us would
be an ungracious host."* Kahlil Gibran

A "Marker Soul" is one who holds the place for another incoming soul for a short period of time. This accounts for unusual amnesia or apparent short-term memory loss. In a Walk-In, generally, the "Marker Soul" does not imprint memories, as we know them, that are generated during the period of time that it inhabits or holds the space in the physical body. Abby's case case was one where a Marker Soul was called into a Braided Soul situation. The female aspect of the Braid was unsure that it wanted to enter into the situation that the male aspect was forced to vacate prematurely. A "Braided-Soul" agreement is sometimes engaged as part of the evolutionary process of Twin Flames. Twin Flames generally hold either the masculine or the feminine aspects of duality. With Twin Flames, it is generally either the male or the female aspects who enters into the body first. Then, at a prearranged time, the souls may choose to switch their roles. Sometimes, the vacating soul may decide to commence life again immediately, either through the vehicle of birth or, more commonly, as a Service Walk-In. The new Transpirant has a period of adjustment while the Twin is still occupying the other body, so the exchange is quite easy, and little, if any, of the body's experience or memory is lost in the process. A braided soul may even integrate together at a later time in the same body, a sort of communal companionship. This link or merging provides expanded psychic awareness but promotes the desire to separate from family or the cultural community. The Merged Soul becomes a mystic.

> *"A sudden gust of wind hit me at that instant and
> made my eyes burn. I stared toward the area in question.
> There was absolutely nothing out of the ordinary.*
> *"I can't see a thing," I said.*
> *"You just felt it," he replied.*
> *"What? The wind?"*
> *"Not just the wind," he said.*
> *"It may seem to be the wind to you,*
> *because the wind is all you know."*
>
> From: <u>Journey to Ixtlan the Lessons of Don Juan</u>, by Carlos Castaneda

Library at Ephesus, Turkey
Photo by Matthew Mitchell

Simultaneous Lifetimes

> "*The temporal sequence is converted into a simultaneous co-existence, the side-by-side existence of things into a state of mutual interpenetration...a living continuum in which time and space are integrated.*" Lama Govinda, a Tibetan monk

It was in the decompression time following one of our most intense classes in hypnotherapy that the following dialogue transpired:

L: "Have you ever thought that you might be someone else at the same time that you are here?"

M: "Yea, I've had an experience like that...I was a bum..." everyone breaks into laughter. "No, seriously!" He has a sense of humor, so he is not upset. "A homeless man in New York I think. He must have been 50. I was there. I was in his body. I saw through his eyes and felt his hunger. It was really scary."

T: "Were you asleep at the time?"

M: "Who, me or the homeless man?"

We are a bit amused, all smiling, by the way that he answers the question. We all like "T" and he knows it. He loves to be teased and to tease, but gently. Like Joey on the sitcom "Friends."

L: "'T' means were you sleeping when you experienced yourself as a homeless man?"

M: "That's what I thought. I don't think so. I was daydreaming, not thinking of anything in particular. And then...there I was, wearing this ragged, brown canvas-like coat, laying in the doorway of some building in an area I'd never dream of walking or driving through now."

L: "So, 'M,' how did you know this was you?"

M: "It was too real. I could even taste what the inside of his mouth tasted like. And it was not good! Not good at all." He fanned in front of his mouth. We all try not to laugh, as we are unsure of his intention. "He was not well. He had dark circles under his eyes, and he drank a lot. He was not happy either. "

T: "So did you get your name?"

M: "No, I didn't get a name. You don't ask yourself your name.

That wouldn't seem right." He looks at "L." "So, did you have an experience like that...with being someone else?"

L: "Yes, I did."

T: "And what happened to you?"

L: "I had a different feeling than 'M.' It was like I was watching this young woman, maybe 22. She had a apartment in Belgium." (Unlike "M," "L" had a great deal of technical background in her experience, but it was less physical in nature. Perhaps just a difference between men and women, or an indication of how differently people, men or women, perceive of life in general.) "I was appalled by her vanity. She was studying to be a hairdresser. She had this sit-down vanity dresser with a huge mirror in her bedroom." She held her arms apart to indicate the size of the mirror. We all laugh at her exaggeration. "Her hair was dyed so black it was blue, and she had these long, red, curved fingernails. And a short, too short, skirt." "L" grabbed the fabric of her own long dress in contrast. "I really did not like this female. She exceeded my boundaries of decency and good taste."

M: "I think I might have liked her." "L" rolled her eyes at him.

L: "I was really judging her. I visited her twice, and each time I was more and more horrified by her drama, her vanity, and her... flakiness. And I knew, I just knew, that this was me...a coexistence." "M" cut in suddenly.

M: "So she was everything that you did not like in other people. But you knew she was you! What a dirty trick." He started to chuckle.

T: "But, 'M,' wasn't it the same in your experience? Wasn't the homeless man what you didn't want to be too?"

M: "Well, would you want to be homeless?"

L: "'M,' you're missing the point. 'T' is trying to point out that these people are living our worst nightmare. I can't imagine ever being flaky..." Everyone laughs because she is more of an intellectual. She continues, "Flaky to that extent, or that vain. I could put up with almost anything but that vanity. She cried for hours over a broken nail or a bad hair day. What a wasted life."

T: "But if they were to experience your lives what would they say about you?"

L: "They probably would not appreciate us either. But it's

hard for me to understand why someone wouldn't want my perfect life." She was grinning, facetiously.

M: "Me either!"

L: "So, 'T,' have you ever had an experience like that? Meeting that Jungian shadow who really lives and breathes."

T: "Well, I'm not sure. I'm not clear that the experience that I had was not to be a future life. I was in the Andes mountains. I lived in an open house, meaning no windows or doors, and I could see snow on the mountain tops in the distance. But it was hot where I was."

L: "Were you a man or a woman?"

T: "A young woman. A Medicine Woman, a healer. She was so contented. And that's all I can remember about it. I just knew that at some point in the present or future I was or would be her. 'R', you've been really quiet, what about you?"

R: "It's just so fascinating. Well, I know who I am elsewhere. I've lived and breathed another experience. I can tap into that life at any time."

M: "So, who is 'R2'?" He chuckled at his cleverness.

R: "Very funny 'M.' Well, I will let you know that I really like this girl. She is about fifteen, very kind, sensitive, yet confident. I had the sense that the universe is grooming her for some type of major political position in the United States government...maybe even President. That will be a tough one for her. I wouldn't want that for anyone."

M: "President, huh?" "M" smiled. "Does she already have a boyfriend?"

R: "I know what you're thinking. No. But my thinking that she will have power, political power, that's not ego at all. It's just an honest knowing. I have to admit, telling you about this makes me uncomfortable, like I am sharing a secret. I know her name, her father's name, the name of her father's company. They have a family company that has been around since the industrial revolution. They own a lot of land, big mansions in the U.S. and abroad, and lots of fancy cars. Including a Rolls Royce. But she is sweet, even if she is a bit spoiled. Her father loves her dearly. She is an only child. Really, that's all want to share." She paused. But, I do talk to her often. She thinks I am an Angel or a friend that no one else can see. So she doesn't let on to anyone when we're together. Like it's our sacred secret. So that's all I want to say." She shrugged her shoulders. Everyone was quiet for a few moments.

L: "I remember someone telling me that she had been contacted telepathically by an Aborigine in Australia who visited her during his Dreamtime. He told her that she was him and he was her; that there was no such thing as time or space to separate them. Just the thought that they were not the same person...which was her thought, not his thought. But over time, she said, she found out that he was right. His life was her life. They were the same soul."

There are several possible explanations for the experiences that these individuals shared. A psychologist might explain that perhaps these experiences were simply metaphorical rather than true, valid experiences. Such metaphors often speak to our psyche to help us to heal our deepest, darkest fears. It was interesting that in "L" and "M's" cases that these co-existent realities were abhorrent to them. But yet in "R's" experience it would seem that the opposite was true. The girl that "R" was aware of seemed to have been born with the proverbial silver spoon in her mouth. Very unlike "R's" experience with life. So it would seem to me that perhaps these co-existent realities represent aspects of the self that are the opposite of what we are or pretend to be. Perhaps these myriad experiences are merely personality masks like those that Joseph Campbell refers to. Or cracked mirrors that reflect what we do not wish our own lives to be. I believe that the soul of each individual aspires for spiritual growth and has the unlimited potential to create whatever the soul needs in order to achieve the growth that it needs. If our Earth is running out of time, perhaps we have accelerated our own process by splitting our own soul into fragments that can gain powerful experiences to bring back to the whole. Or maybe we gained the awareness that the ancients have always believed, that we are indeed all one and the same person. Perhaps it is just our perception that separates us.

Renewing the Contract for Life

I thought that I had just experienced a vivid dream. Now I know it was not just a dream, but an alternate reality or glimpse into a probable future event. This is what happened. I was looking at the calendar on the wall. (In my dream.) It was only October; October of 1997, but the calendar was turned to February of 1998. The 26th was was circled (by me?) in red three times like a bull's eye or target. I saw myself driving my car home from work. I was adjusting the radio station. Out in the country there is quite a big curve in the road. I watched as the small sport's car I was driving (and at that time owned) skidded out of control on an icy patch and crashed in slow motion. I watched my body as it was slammed from one side into the door, and then the car flipped completely over crushing me. I knew, as all dying people must at some point recognize, that there is no turning back in on the body, there is only going out. I knew the damage was too great, irreparable. There was too much blood lost. I watched my soul lift from the body, and the body slumped in death within seconds afterward. I was completely detached from the event. There was absolutely no fear, only a strange thought: "Oh, so that is how I planned it this time." I was aware somehow that it took more than twenty minutes before rescue vehicles could reach the scene. No one else was involved in the accident and I remember being grateful for that. "Good planning" I thought to myself, as if with approval.

But then there was this voice. A voice I remembered hearing somewhere before in my distant past. A voice that I recognized. Definitely a male voice. The voice said to me in my dream state, "Is this what you really want to do? You don't have to you know."

I remember asking "What?"

Then there was the answer, firmly and directly: "This is what you planned, but you can stay longer if you'd like."

I remember asking how much longer, as if longer was not such a good deal.

"As long as you'd like. Really you can," the voice replied.

I remember looking at the faces of my family members and think-

---

ing that I was still needed by them, especially the children. They would be okay, but better off if I stuck around for awhile longer. I did not want to put them through this. Then this mental debate took place somewhere in a corner of my head. It was as if my soul, body, and mind were negotiating a length of time for an extension of life that would be most appropriate. They all agreed upon twenty years, as if it was the picking of a lottery number. A part of me, but I'm not certain if it was the logical or emotional part, was surprised that that was the agreed-upon number. Not twenty-one or two, but twenty. Exactly twenty.

"How about twenty years?" I asked the Voice. "But what do I have to do to earn them?" I knew there had to be some catch, and I wanted to know who I was dealing with.

"You can have twenty years, and if you want more or less we can arrange it...there is no catch. Well, not the catch you think. This is okay. Trust me. We only ask that you continue with your work with others for awhile longer. Those Walk-ins who are allowed to renegotiate are always asked to continue in their service if they have found it. And you have."

"But what should I do?" I asked.

The Voice softly chuckled and then replied, "If I were you, I'd sell that car."

I traded in the car within a week, asking that all future drivers be safe in it. I now celebrate every February 26th as if it were my new birthday.

Kinds of Human Death

"Our human death is, simply speaking, nothing other than suicide. We human beings, because of our potentially free consciousness and free ability to change ourselves, are choosing our own destinies, whether we are aware of it or not. When, how, and where we are going to die are being determined by various accumulated factors--physical and mental, spiritual and social--which we are causing ourselves to experience through our own way of life."[2]

According to Michio Kushi, there are seven methods of death that we may choose to end our physical existence: *Biological Death, Psychological Death, Social Death, Accidental Death, Ideological Death, Natural Death, and Spiritual Death.*

Biological Death is the result of mental and physical diseases. In modern society, Kushi believes that the majority of deaths occur in this category. However, since disease is a result of neglect or poor dietary practices, we fall out of harmony with our environment, and our physical and mental conditions become incapable of sustaining our life force.

Psychological Death involves the creation of psychological delusions and drama which motivates the premature termination of life. Loss of a sense of joy and happiness in life motivates the creation of such delusions. This method is becoming more popular with younger generations.

Social Death: Every century, millions of people die as a result of what they believe to be justified warfare. It is a chosen method of death for a social cause.

Accidental Death: Accidents occur when our physical, mental, and spiritual perceptions are obscured by an unhealthy way of life. Carelessness, over excitement, and lack of clear judgment are causes of accidental death. However directly or indirectly we create accidents by our lack of attention to life.

2. Kushi, Michio, The book of Macrobiotics, The Universal Way of Health and Happiness, Japan Publications, Inc.,1977, p.112

Ideological Death is viewed as an apology or taking responsibility for an action that we may have taken against society or others. "Seppuku-harakiri" or self-termination of life traditionally done by Japanese samurai is an example of this.

Natural Death is a prolonged state of existence where the body eventually withers like an old tree and dies. Such Elders have great wisdom, a deep appreciation of life, and accept death as a natural process.

Spiritual Death is a self-initiated vibrational shift into a higher state or world. Such a person disappears at their own will. It is considered to be the most elevated form of death.

Paris
Photo by Shauna Angel Blue

A Soul's Letter to a Borrowed Body

It is time that I formally introduce myself to you and apologize for not doing so earlier. I did not know who I was or what I was doing here until recently. I had always thought for some reason that we were at odds with each other, that you were somehow an enemy that could not be trusted and must be managed or thwarted. I thought that I could not depend upon you for the long haul, to complete this mission that burned like rocket fuel in my tireless soul. But time and time again, you have proven to be a worthy advocate of this Earthly assignment, embracing, holding ground, and then climbing with greater fury than I could ever imagine possible. Even when I betrayed and robbed you of your precious sleep, you rallied tirelessly to my defense, like the ancient sword Excalliber did for the crusading King Arthur of Camelot. I betrayed you first in the recklessness of my youth and then again and again in relentless passion for more of life than can be rightfully smuggled into the perimeters of one mere day. I have not fed you well, groomed you nearly often enough, nurtured your health, nor encouraged you by admitting your unique beauty and strength that far exceeds the notion of popular human definition. For are we not all who wear these physical forms merely mirror-like reflections of our own Divine Creator? Who could judge us so harshly as to say which image of the Earth Mask is the most Divinely Inspired? We are all, as they say, Stardust and Golden. This face holds furrows of wisdom and the scars of faith.

And so I am here my Friend, to tell you now how much I honor and appreciate all that you have made possible in my own experience in this existence, and all others where I have failed to do so in the distant past. Our marriage may not be one that you have chosen. But whether it is God, Fate, or some Immortal Plan that has brought us to the threshold of the vast Circle of life and death, we are partners or co-conspirators in this great inspiration called life. And while we may fail to estimate the significance of what we are doing here, we must trust that time will reveal the Greater Plan to all of us who choose to wrap our Sacred Souls with such Divine Cloth. For deep within our cells is hidden the encrypted message that has maintained and sustained human life upon this planet. The Body is the secret of the

Ancient Mariner undiscovered yet, like a prisoner held in the bottle of a vast ocean; or the secret chamber of mysteries nestled securely in the paws of the Egyptian Sphinx. Our bodies heal us, hold us, and teach us compassion by shedding uncounted tears of joy and sorrow, pain and ecstasy. You may not have asked for me, but I am here, and together we forge a new history. Like a two-cord rope, we are not easily broken, and when it is time to leave you, I shall do so with humble reverence. We have walked a lifetime of miles together, forged streams, and scaled mountains in search of the Holy Grail. At the end of this journey, I have found the Grail in You. You are the Living Vessel of this Eternal Soul, Holy and Divine.

Door at Bath
Photo by Shauna Angel Blue

From: *Mansions of the Soul, The Cosmic Conception*

Written in 1930 by H. Spencer Lewis

"The sacred scriptures of all religions speak of only one earth, one globe, one place in the whole of the universe where (hu)man was created and exists as an image of some Divine Creator. Science, on the other hand, busily occupies itself on the borderline of discovery, anticipating that it may reveal to us at any moment the actual existence of other planets than this one, filled with human life or living creatures not unlike ourselves. The gospels of the ages and of all nations speak of great Avatars and messengers of the Holy Messiah and the God of Gods, who have come to earth to save all living beings. Is there no redemption, no saving grace, for the beings on other planets, or have they no souls, no personalities that are Divine and worthy of Infinite consideration?

"Is this personality of ours, this individuality which we strive to build up through idealism and the elimination of undesirable traits, merely a temporary or imaginary creation of our minds?

"Down through the ages has come the cry for Light and more Light. About us, everything is changing and nothing seems permanent and fixed. The mountains crumble away, the rivers dry up and cease to flow, islands sink, and new seas are formed. The great oaks, in all their majesty, must succumb to transition, to change, or death. (Humans) go on their way and cross the borderline into the unknown and seem to end their existence in the twinkling of an eye. Is there any part of man, therefore, or any part of nature, that is immortal, unchanging, permanent, and continuous?

"Is there a survival beyond (humanity's) mere memory of the personalities that now exist in human form? Will the death of the body or the change of its form release an intangible and invisible something that will rise to greater heights than the monuments to remembered characters, or surmount the limitations of Time and Space, and thereby attain incorruptibility and immortality?

"If the present physical body is a Mansion of the Soul and the Great Messenger of God went forward to prepare other places for the Soul, are there other Mansions to be attained, and how?

"It has been the hope of the world--and the inspiring power that

has enabled (Humanity) to carry on in the face of mighty obstacles--that some day they might be freed of the mortal cloak that enslaves them on this earth and rise to a life of eternal bliss and goodness. If the religions that have inspired humanity are true and the culminating joy of this life is to be found only in the spiritual existence of this Soul in a realm beyond the earth, why have the Souls of millions been imprisoned here to suffer and to know torment, sorrow, strife, and conflict? What end is served, what mission fulfilled, by the incarnation of the Soul here? If, out of the sublime, spiritual consciousness of a blissful kingdom comes each Soul, and to this same high state must it return to enjoy its Divine heritage, why is it sent forth from such a transcendental place to dwell in association with corruption, sin, evil, and dross?

"These are questions which millions are asking today and which must be answered more completely, more satisfyingly, and more constructively than they have been answered in the past. Directing our attention to the worship of a God, and enthusing us with the belief that this God is loving, merciful, tender, and just, will not answer these questions but merely add to the mystery of our existence. Granted that an omnipotent, all-wise, merciful, and loving God created us and directed into these physical bodies a part of God's Soul Consciousness to suffer and to endure the trials and tribulations of unknown and unexpected experiences here on earth, still the question remains, 'Why are we here?' and 'How are mercy, love, and justice made manifest in such a plan?'"[3]

The song that I came to sing remains unsung to this day.
I have spent my days in stringing and in unstringing my instrument.
The time has not yet come true, the words have not been rightly set;
only there is the agony of wishing in my heart.
The blossom has not opened; only the wind is sighing by.
I have not seen his face, nor have I listened to his voice;
Only have I heard his gentle footsteps from the road before my house.
I live in the hope of meeting with him;
but this meeting is not yet.   by Rabindranath Tagore

---

3. H. Spencer Lewis, Mansions of the Soul, The Cosmic Connection, San Jose California, 1930, The Rosicrucian Press, LTD. pp. 18-21

Other Mansions, Other Worlds

> *"Who is the creator you ask? We have existed before time began. We will always exist. We never die."* Joseph answered.

"I'm playing with my friend Jason Waller," Joseph began. *"We are going up the steps, and it's dark in the stairway. It's darker upstairs, where the toys are. I think it's always like that. Even though it's daytime. We're playing with trucks."*

"Joseph," I said, *I want you to ahead, to a half hour before the event occurred. The event that created your allergies."*

"Still there. Still playing."

"I want you to be aware of everything around you." I was thinking allergens, dust, anything that may have created allergies. *I want you to go to the critical event now, noticing everything..."* I noticed his face was changing. He was smiling.

"Yes, I see it happening." And then he was silent. Completely silent.

The Beginning: Session One

"My idea of hell is my eyes and nose running all the time. Just like they have most of my life." Joseph was serious, his dark eyebrows drew closer together like a draw-bridge closing quickly to trap a thought. "When I was at home, on the farm, in the morning when I woke up my head was always full and my eyes were glued shut. When I went away to school, college, it got better. Then I had allergy tests and shots." He sipped his tea and looked up at me. "So now I'm ready to try something else. That's why I'm here." He seemed to be acquainted with the nature of my Age Regression Therapy work, and was anxious to get right into the session. I instructed Joseph to walk down the corridor of his life until he came to an open door. This door represented the time that the root cause for his allergies, the "critical event" as we call it, existed. "On the open door, there is a number. This number represents the age that you were when when the critical event occurred." I then asked, "What is the number on the door Joseph?"

He rubbed the side of his nose with his index finger. Hesitantly he answered, "Seven. The door has the number seven on it."

"Good. Now, I want you to step in through that door. Easily and effortlessly, you do so. You notice how the time is different, how you are different. You are in your past. You are aware of the clothing that you are wearing. What are you wearing?

"A kind of brown and blue stripe T-shirt with a blue knit collar. Patched-knee blue jeans."

"Good." I was surprised at his attention to detail. "And are you inside or outside?"

"Inside. But not at home. At a friend's house."

"What is happening?" I asked.

"I'm playing with my friend Jason Waller," Joseph began. "We are going up the steps, and it's dark in the stairway. It's darker upstairs, where the toys are. I think it's always like that. Even though it's daytime. We're playing with trucks."

"Joseph," I said, I want you to move ahead, to a half hour before the event occurred. The event that created your allergies."

"Still there. Still playing."

"I want you to be aware of everything around you." I was thinking allergens, dust, anything that may have created allergies. I want you to go to the critical event now, noticing everything..." I noticed his face was changing. He was smiling.

"Yes, I see it happening." And then he was silent. Completely silent. When he spoke again, it was in whispers. "It's like a shadow of me...some kind of ghost-like presence that stands up, arches the back, arms outstretched. But the body keeps pushing the truck, making the truck noises. Playing. Like it is on automatic pilot. I...the soul in the body...I think I leave there. Leave the body. There is someone else in the body. Someone who is very confused about being there." He stops speaking, thinking, the brows drawn together again. He is analyzing.

I knew that I had to shift him from this thoughts. "Let go of all of your thoughts, Joseph and just be aware. Aware of what happens next. What happens next?" I ask.

"I want back in. There is a kind of battle over the body. An Armageddon of sorts. I realize that I am...victorious. I am back."

"How long have you been gone, Joseph?"

"The body is twelve now."

"And where does the battle take place?"

"It's not like that. It's not like a real war. It's more of a spiritual battle. It reminds me of the story of how Jacob battled the angel on the riverbank, but the wrestling took place only with the spirits. I can see the body standing in the front yard, and the dog beside the body. The dog is growling, looking up at the spirits. Dog doesn't like what is going on."

"So where was your...spirit for those five years?"

"The reexchange was suppose to have taken place in four years, but it didn't happen until five. Because he...wouldn't give up the body. He liked it there."

"And the spirit...the one you are fighting with over the body, Joseph. What was the name of that spirit?"

"Ralph." He smiles. "What a funny name, Ralph."

"And where did Ralph come from?" I asked.

"Out there." He slowly lifts his index finger toward the ceiling, a mute gesture. "I want to say that he is..." he hesitates. "I think he...was not from here, nor from where I was from." I can tell that he is thinking again.

"And where are you from?" I ask.

Joseph starts to sputter out letters, spelling. "H-a-i-d, no 't'-i-e-s. Haities. Pronounced 'Hay-at-dease.'

I am wondering if he means "Pleiades", the Seven Sisters. Did he mistake the "P" for an "H"? How do I ask without leading. "Would you pronounce the name again for me?" I ask.

He says the same once again: "Hay-at-dease."

"What is the first letter?" I ask.

"H. Definitely not a 'P.' It's not 'Pleiades'. I thought it might be, but it's not." He answered my question.

"So where is Haities?" I ask.

Once again he just gestured. "Out there. It's not on any star chart. Never will be. But it is a physical reality. It does exist."

"Did you know Ralph before this...event took place?" I asked.

"It's called a reexchange. And yes. I did."

"How did you know him?"

"I met him before. But he's not from Haities. We had a...contract of sorts."

"Tell me about Haities. What is it like?" I ask.

"Monks. We look like monks. Androgynous, not really male or female. We are in these...containers, lined up triangular, like bowling pins in a bowling alley. Only we don't look like bowling pins.

We look, kind of A-framed with the top of the...container, body, whatever...kind of rounded, like where the head is. The faces are there, on the outside of the container, like they have been painted on. We look very surreal, lined up like that. We can hear each other's thoughts."

"And what are you all doing there?" I asked.

"Waiting." He sighed deeply, remembering a faint feeling. "Waiting our turn."

"Your turn for what?" I asked.

"Our turn to go to the next place." He spelled again, "L-o-o-m... Loominous."

"And what is Loominous like?"

He smiled slowly. "It is like what they call the Garden of Eden. It's lush, green, beautiful, tranquil. Everyone is happy there all the time. The bodies there are different from Earth. The bodies never die. We just shift in and out of them as we need them. Everyone is peaceful. Until they are ready to go again. They stay as long as they want. To revitalize. And when they are ready for their assignments, they approach the Planners."

"Planners?"

"Yeah. The Planners help us decide where to go next, to serve. That is what we do. We serve where and when we are needed."

"How many serve?"

"There are fourteen hundred and forty here on this planet, on Earth now. There are others...on other planets. Two thousand eighty of us in total."

I wanted to ask ten questions at one time. I settled for, "How many times have you come here? To Earth?"

"Five hundred and sixty-seven different bodies. Lifetimes. On

Earth."

"Can you talk to these 'Planners'?" I asked.

"Yes." He paused. "There are seven. I have seven Planners."

"Are these 'Planners' just yours, or do they help others?"

"They help others as well, but there are other Planners too. These seven happen to be mine. Always have been, always will be."

"Is there another name for these Planners?" I ask.

"No. Just Planners."

"So..." I hesitate. "Who is the Creator?"

"Who is the Creator?" He pauses. "We have existed before time began. We will always exist. We never die."

"So why," I ask, "Are Human Beings afraid to die?"

"Because they are...not us. They think that their bodies are all that exist because they are taught this from an early age. We know differently. The fourteen hundred forty of us are not at all afraid of death. It is how we get back to Haities and then on to Loominous. We do our job and go home for awhile. That's our perspective. We go there when the body sleeps too."

"Which place do you like best, Joseph?"

"Loominous, of course." He smiles as if I have asked a ridiculous question. "Haities is like...a processing place. A between times. An interval. We wait there. Nothing more. Wait to move on when it's our turn to go to Loominous."

I suddenly remember, as time is running out, that we are in session to discover the reason for his allergies. "So, Joseph, what did this...process have to do with your allergies?"

He sighed once again. "It was Ralph...he was trying to make changes in the body. He messed with something in the body and I couldn't correct it. It was like faulty wiring. He short-circuited something."

"Why did he do this?" I asked.

"Because he didn't know any better. And he wouldn't give up the body at the time that the contract was up. I had to evict him."

"If he was from your planet, wasn't he...more evolved than that?"

"No, he wasn't from my planet." Joseph smiled. "Not every...one...is evolved. We have an evolved purpose, but not every...one is as evolved on Haities. But on Loominous they have to be to get there."

"And is there someone in charge of Loominous?" I ask.

"Yes...there is the 'Grandmother' of us all."

"And what does she do?" I ask.

"She..." he chokes a bit, remembering. "She...nurtures us and makes certain that we have enough love. That gets us ready for the next lifetime."

I am aware that it is time for the session to end. "Is there anything else that you need to know at this time?" I ask him.

"No. He hesitates. But can I tell you something? About you?"

"Of course Joseph. What is it?"

"You are one of us." He gently shifts his weight in the chair. "You can bring me back now." And so I do.

Session Two

> "My life is my message." Mohandas Gandhi

It has been only a few short days since my last session with Joseph. He seems reflective as we speak about his week and review our last session. What surprises me most about Joseph and his experience is that he appears to be an extremely conservative, quiet individual. I wonder if he is having a bit of difficulty accepting the information obtained from the last session.

"You know, in one way, all of this somehow makes sense to me."

Joseph sets down his tea cup and glances up at me. He is wearing a navy blue Polo knit shirt and khaki slacks. There was a time in my life when my memories were really fuzzy. I'm not sure that what I do remember other people told me."

"Like what?" I ask him.

"Well, it seems that there were some things involving discipline during that time. I think that something changed. The doctor told my parents that a lot of the problem had to do with my allergies bothering...aggravating me."

"But now what do you think?" I ask.

"I think that this process was going on, the..."he pauses not certain what to call it.

"Soul exchange?"

"Yes. Do you really believe that it happened that way? I mean, you must run into strange stuff once in awhile, don't you?" Joseph leans forward in his chair, fingers laced, hands resting on his knees.

I smile at him. "It is interesting work. I never question anyone's experience, and if a client has difficulty accepting what may have happened, I tell them that whatever has come forward was in their subconscious mind for a reason. Something needs to be healed, and the mind simply brings forward what we need to know or be aware of to heal it, in a way that can be considered truth or a metaphor by the individual."

"What do you mean, 'truth or a metaphor'? Are you saying that my experience may not be real? I have a hard time believing that I even have enough imagination to create what I told you in the last session. It seems more like science fiction, and I have always hated science fiction stuff. Never watch it and never read it."

"No, that is not what I meant, Joseph. I am just saying that sometimes people have difficulty believing what a session may reveal to them. Let's take abuse for example. This is purely fictional, but an example. A woman is abused by her father when she is five. Now, at age thirty, she starts to dream about a lion. She sees herself walking with the lion, and feels that a part of her loves the lion, but she is afraid that at any moment the lion may attack her and hurt her. The dreams make her more and more anxious in her waking life and begins to affect her job, her health; lets say she develops anxiety attacks...and this affects all aspects of her life. In her despair, her doctor may refer her to a hypnotherapist. In the regression, she sees herself in her room playing with the lion. She loves the lion, but is afraid that he will hurt her at any moment. Now we know that most people do not have lions in their room, so we need to find out who or what the lion really is. A good therapist may think they know who the lion is, but will never reveal what they think. They allow the session to reveal the eventual truth, if not then, then maybe the next time. The proof is always in the healing, and the healing generally occurs when the truth is revealed and the fences mended."

He smiles at me. "So we will find out in this session whether my friend 'Ralph' was really from out there." He points his finger to the ceiling.

"Is Ralph a friend?" I smile at him.

"It doesn't seem like it," he sighed.

We reviewed any questions that he might have concerning the session. I asked him what, if anything, he wanted me to ask or affirm during the session. "Any post-hypnotic suggestions that you would like?"

"Well, you know, I would really like to know what I need to do to heal these allergies. They are better, by the way. Can you give them the suggestion to just go away?" He laughs and moves to the beige recliner in the corner of my therapy room.

After a short induction, I ask Joseph to return to the time that the reason for his allergies was created. Once again, he is in the same room, playing trucks with his friend. He is seven years old. "I want you to be aware, Joseph, of everything that is happening around you. Listen. What do you hear?"

"Just us, making that truck noise with our lips and our breath." He shifts his weight in the chair.

"And what happens next?" I ask him.

Well, there is a funnel-like energy above my head. I see some swirling light, energy, whatever you want to call it, coming out of the top of the funnel. Then something that looks the same goes back in. It's like seeing your breath in winter," he whispers.

"Do the boys see this happen." I ask him.

"No, they just keep playing. Oblivious. but it seems like I am looking at them from far away now."

"Where are you, Joseph?"

"Loominous. No, I go to Haities first, but it's just like touching first base and going on to the next."

"Do you see what is going on with your body when you are there?"

"No," he answers, "but I am aware somehow of what is going on there."

"And where did the other energy come from that went into the body?" I ask him.

"He...it, was not from the same place that we are from. He's from some other place, but definitely not Earth." He is silent for a few moments. "I think he came here on a spaceship or some sort. We don't need spaceships to get where we are going. None of us are like those gray alien beings. Nothing like that. Not even close. In four years I came back, when the body was eleven. But he wouldn't give it up right away. It took nearly a year to reclaim it."

"Ralph?" I ask.

"Ralph stands for something else. Where he was from, or, no, the name of our contract for him to come in for the experience."

"So how did you find the body again, when it was time to return?"

"It is kind of like a homing device to the mind, but much different. That is as close as I can come to explain it in our terms."

"Is that how you are born initially to the body?" I wonder.

"I'm seeing how this happens, but I don't know how to explain it." *He pauses.* "There is this...Power." *He stops.* "A group of, well, the best description I can give you is not right or even close. There is is this group of Powers, I see them like...benevolent nuns, who prepare the space for the soul to enter. Each group of souls has its own Powers who do this for them. These Powers are not us, but attached to us in this function. They only prepare the way for us. And then we come in with the first breath of the living body. When we are called in to service. But we only serve activities of the Light, whether it's volunteer work, like helping someone move, or teaching, or helping others. That's what we come here for."

"And do other souls or energies come from other places or other planets?" *I ask.*

"Of course, but they have different intentions. Some are trouble-makers."

"And where are they from?" *I lean forward. His voice seems suddenly more quiet.*

"I want to say Orion, but I'm not sure." *His eyelids flutter.* "It seems like I knew everything that was supposed to happen to the body before I was born, like a great Plan of some sort. And while I was gone, when I came back, I already knew that I had a new baby brother and sister."

"How did your body feel when you came back to it?"

"I had to do some adjusting. Just like when someone else drives your car and you have to adjust the seat and the mirrors. The body was bigger too, I had to get used to that. It was like hearing noises in your car that you did not hear before."

"And what about the allergies, Joseph?"

"They were a side effect of the changes that the other one had made."

"Can this now be healed?" I ask him.

"Yes and no. There are some things that I can do, like a catalyst to create change, but there are a few things that are irreparable. I need to accept this body for one thing. It seems that I haven't really done that since I returned. And I need to let go of my anger at that other one, Ralph. I think I felt like a victim, even though I was victorious eventually."

"Would you like to talk to Ralph, to tell him how you feel about what he did?"

"I think I dealt with Ralph pretty much. We just aren't used to our contracts being violated. It's the betrayal. If he hadn't left, the body might have expired. He was jeopardizing my work, and putting the body at risk. His staying too long took its toll. None of us expected him to do that. He won't get another chance with us. He'll have to go somewhere else."

"What was Ralph's purpose, in coming to Earth?" I wondered.

"To learn. That is the group that talks about Earth as being a Schoolhouse, where lessons need to be learned."

"So, do you want to forgive Ralph?"

"I suppose I could do that. It was part of his learning process, that's all. Ralph, wherever you are now, I forgive you for what you did." He took a deep breath.

"Now," I said, "Take a deep breath and as you exhale, let go of any feelings or energies that are no longer serving your highest good. Let them go to the Highest Light. Release them. And when you are free, make certain that the body is also free. Where did you store this experience in the body?"

"In my gut, my intestines," he responded quickly.

"Are you ready to release any suffering, pain, or any emotions stored in your intestines?" He nods. "Then take a deep breath or two and do that. Release and let go. Feel, sense, and know that it is happening."

He takes three deep breaths, and then rests quietly.

"Joseph, is everything clear?"

"Yes."

"Then do whatever else you need to heal your allergies. Take the time you need and then let me know when you are done."

"I'm done." He pauses and then goes on. "You know, some of us forget for awhile why we have come here. We get caught up in material things...money, cars, the stock market, love..." he smiles. "But we always get back to it. We always do what we have come here to do. We can't help ourselves from helping. It is inevitable. We may get caught up in life and material things for awhile, but we always end up helping others in the end. I guess it's sort of like what Gandhi said, 'my life is my message'."

Note: It has been three years. Joseph has been fairly clear of his allergies since our second session. He left his traditional job and now helps others full time.

The Cosmic Planners

Time and time again, I have encountered in Regression Therapy the notion of those who assist a soul in the process of planning their next incarnation. They also may assist in the review process immediately following death, for that is a larger part of the assessment in reviewing the damages: the karmic mistakes that the soul may feel they made during their walk on Earth. While there may be one or three or seven or twelve "Planners" who make themselves known to the client during a session, there is generally only one or possibly two who will actually communicate with them. I encourage the client to ask pertinent questions concerning their Path; such questions which may allow them to gain a greater understanding of their Soul's Purpose. The client must be prepared to accept the information as it is shared.

If a person seems to need a visit with their Planners due to confusion in their life or a lack of clarity during a session, I encourage them to seek the Planners out. My particular technique is to embrace the process by allowing the client to see, sense, or feel that there are seven Golden Steps before them. The process of climbing the steps slowly allows them to raise their vibratory frequency at a comfortable level. This increase in frequency has nothing to do with brain-wave function; it is a matter of calibrating the spirit to be able to communicate on the Higher Plane with their Higher Guides or Higher Self. One is reaching for a Higher Plane of Existence. Once they are there, I ask them to step off onto the floor of this Higher Place. They are met by those who have been waiting for them. I ask them, how many are there? Then I encourage them to ask who they are. Many times the Planners call themselves "Ones Who Help You." But at other times, specific names may be shared. I then ask the client to review with the Planners the Blueprint of their life that is there on the table. They may ask questions pertaining to their past or present, but most of the time Planners will not answer questions for another person or persons, and are most hesitant to reveal future events. They also will not tell a person what to do, as that tends to strip away the free will of the individual. Planners are most helpful in illuminating the nature of this Earth's Journey and Soul's Purpose. They are useful to assist one in getting back on track and staying there. A client once inquired of a Planner if the Planner had ever been human. In that particular case the answer was a hesitant "no." The same client also asked about the reason one might want to function as a Planner. The answer was quite simply, "This is what we do. We exist to serve." It would seem that everyone on Earth should be aware that such assistance as the Planners exist as they could be most helpful in directing the course of our lives. I have found that this is not the case for two reasons: Planners are not always that easy to access, as it seems that one must be spiritually prepared to encounter them. Also, they will not offer any guidance unless they are asked specific questions.

Door at Tor, Glastenbury England
Photo by Shauna Angel Blue

The Seventh Plane

"Is there a Heaven?"
"Oh yea, it's the place where dreams come true."
"Maybe this is Heaven." From the Movie, *"Field of Dreams"*

"Did I tell you that I burned a hole in my carpet?" Mary asked casually.

"No, how did you do that, I asked." We had been talking for ten minutes.

"Burning his pictures. I had a tray, and had such a hot fire going that I didn't even think about the carpet underneath. It burnt a hole right through." It was a painful chuckle that followed. "I want to know more, though..." her voice trailed off as she reflected about her childhood and the abuse she suffered from her paternal grandfather. "I was talking with my oldest sister, Theresa, and she told me that the reason that she, Theresa, was sick all of the time was after he had been...with her." She paused and looked down, pushing the band on her left finger with the thumb of her right hand.

"And your mother?" I stopped. "She never knew what was going on?"

"If she did, she sure never let on. I think she just didn't care. It was...or would have been... too much for her to deal with. I mean, she had seven kids, a full-time job, and a drunk for a husband. It kept her overwhelmed just with that. Of course, all she cared about was the boys anyway. We three girls were...invisible." Tears welled up in her eyes. But somehow, all that bothers me now is my two sister's pain. I wonder if they will survive it. I don't know how to explain it, but..." she suddenly stopped talking and stared into the corner of the room.

"But what, Mary?"

"But. I don't really know if I want to tell you this."

"If it makes you uncomfortable, you don't have to explain."

"No, I really do. That's why I'm here, actually. I don't know what to do. It's my marriage... She gazed up at me, blue-green eyes breaking with her face into a slight smile. "He...my husband, Tony, he's not happy with some of the ways that I've changed."

"Mary, are you happy with some of the ways that you've changed?"

"My life seems to have a deeper meaning, and he's not the center of it. He never wanted kids, and I think it's because he would have been jealous. I know that is true. But, then again, I never pushed because at the time, it wasn't that important."

"Is it important to you now?" I asked her.

"No, that's not it. That's not what's bothering him. We aren't getting along because I've changed. He tells me all the time I'm not the Mary, the woman, he married. And he's right. I just really don't care about his short-sited dreams anymore." She looked down at her hiking boots.

"Did you care about his dreams before, Mary?"

"Of course. Whatever he wanted...his old car, his drinking buddies, his fishing and hunting trips. It was just like when I was a kid growing up...whatever Dad or the boys wanted...that was all that mattered. We girls and Mom, we were like second rate beings. I sound like I am still angry, but I don't think it bothers me like it used to. Now I just think that distorted part of the whole scenario was ridiculous. Like the 'Emperor's New Clothes' type of ridiculous. We females were all duped by them. Now I don't know if it was a cultural bias or my family curse. Probably the latter."

"So what happened when you got married?" I asked.

"I transferred that curse to my marriage. It was like I married my own father. And of course, my husband ate it up. That's why he married me I think. For ten years he took advantage of me. Or I should say, I allowed it. And now, when I'm not there, dressed to greet him at the door with a drink and a kiss when he gets home from work, he comes unglued. Never mind that I have no life of my own."

"Mary, did you have a job outside of the home?"

"Yes, but now just part-time. My jobs always had to fit his schedule. I was offered a huge promotion with our company a year ago, but it meant that I had to travel, to work full-time, and he had a fit. I turned down a twenty-five thousand dollar a year opportunity. And he complains about money all of the time, how I spend too much on the house, or on groceries. None of his behavior makes sense to me now. It's like I am seeing this man for the first time, and I don't like the way that he treats his wife, more like a slave."

"Mary, do you still love your husband?" I asked her.

She looked up at me, a bit startled by my question perhaps. "I don't think I ever did, but it never bothered me before. I must have been asleep or maybe I was dead inside. Now I feel this great urgency to do something more meaningful with my life...I want to go back to school, but he says, in a very demonstrative way, that he will not allow it. But now his tirades just don't bother me. I ignore him. I never could before." She reached into her backpack and handed me a picture. "This is important to me now." It was a picture of a group of smiling children in front of the Field Museum of Natural History.

"Are you drawn to be with children?' I asked quietly.

"I really want to teach. I want to do what ever I have to do to go back to school and finish my degree. It would only take a year total, with student teaching." She was animated. "See this one?" She pointed to a little girl in the front row. "She lights up whenever I come into the room. She calls me Mater." She giggled and pointed to a woman in the picture. "This is Sister Fran. She lets me volunteer at the school. This was a field trip. We had a ball! But I was late getting home, and Tony wasn't happy with me at all. I told him where I was, with Sister Fran, but that didn't matter. I just wasn't with him. He told me I couldn't help at the school anymore. I walked two miles to get there on Mondays and Wednesdays." Her smile faded like evening light.

"And why doesn't he want you to go back to school?' I wondered, fearing I already knew the answer to that question.

She slid the picture back into her purse. "He says we don't have the money for something I'll never use. But the truth is, I think he's afraid I will teach, and then I won't depend upon him for every nickel. Or he's afraid I won't be home all the time where he wants me to be. You know, I had to ask a friend for a ride here. The only places out of town that I go are pretty much where he takes me. He drops me off at work on Tuesday, Thursday, and Friday, but I walk home at three. We have another car...it's Tony's '57 Chevy, but I'm not allowed to drive it. It's just an expensive hobby of his. My life is changing, Dr. Mitchell; changing fast, and I'm not sure how to handle these changes. I've applied for student loans for next September, and I'm ready to go. Except for...Tony. What do you think I should do?"

"Mary, how do you think Tony will react when you tell him?"

"Well," she smiled, "He's never hit me, never laid a hand on me. Not that he hasn't wanted to, especially in the past few months."

"What do you want to do?" I ask.

"I think I want, will need, a divorce. There is no one else, no other man; no, not at all. I just don't want to be married anymore, for several reasons. I know Tony. It just isn't going to work...with me having a career that I love." She looked at her feet once again. "The truth is, I want to pour my all into my teaching, and there won't be much left for Tony. Not enough for him, that is. I know he won't settle for that. He won't be happy. Not after the way that it's been these past years. Everything will change in his little world, and he doesn't do change well."

I smiled at her. "Change creates a lot of fear, but it is inevitable. The one true constant in life is change. Isn't it time that you allowed yourself the luxury of owning your own dreams?"

"Yes," she replied, tears streaming down her face. "But Tony is a good man. I don't really want to hurt him. Intentionally that is. It's just that I know I have to do this." I handed her a tissue for her tears. She stopped talking abruptly and looked right into my eyes. "Do you believe in dreams? I mean, not the kind we are talking about, because I think you must be really living your dream, helping people; I mean dreams you have when you're asleep. Do you think that dreams can affect you?" She looked up at me, and I suddenly became aware of the real reason she had found her way to my office.

"Yes, of course. Do you need me to tell you about the power of dreams from a psychological standpoint? They say that dreams can be the subconscious mind expressing itself when it is not free to do so otherwise." I watched her blush. "Or, are these dreams a more...metaphysical or spiritual?"

She smiled. "Dreams about Angels." She corrected herself, "Or I should say dreams about just one Angel in particular. Do you want to hear about them? I really haven't really told anyone." She looked at her feet again. "Who could I tell?"

"You can tell me if you want to."

"There were three dreams, maybe more, but three is all that I remember for certain. In the first dream, I was wandering, like I was lost, through this huge, Victorian Mansion. I came to a large, ornately carved door. I knew that I had to open the door, but when I did, there was a pulsing bright light on the other side. The light was all that I could see at first, but when my eyes got used to it, I saw a tall, thin person standing there. I couldn't tell whether it was a man or a woman, but they did look strangely familiar. I heard a dog bark outside, so I woke up, and kind of forgot all about the dream until I went to bed the next night. In my next dream, I was walking through what looked more like a Frank Lloyd Wright house. The strange part is that it had a real stream, with rocks and the whole bit, running right through the middle of it. As I followed along the stream, I remember thinking how smooth the stones were, like the stream had been running there for thousands of years. The house, too, was very old, and it looked like someone had been working on it here and there. I saw an old stone arched doorway at the end of the house, and then I saw that same bright light was there again, like in my dream before." She stopped talking for a moment. "And then it spoke to me. Or not really spoke, but somehow I knew what it was saying to me. I was trying so hard to remember what it was saying, but I knew my mind was forgetting. It was like you want to hold a thought but you can't, it escapes you into some great void." She laughed quietly. "Now you must think I'm really nuts." She smiled.

"No, not at all. Not at all. Just fascinated." I smiled back at her. "And what happened in the third dream."

She was smoothing the velvet of the couch gently with her small hand, as if soothing her own spirit in the process. "It was nearly two weeks later. I was walking in a house that looked like most of it was made with glass. I felt sheltered, but all around me there was nature. Even birds were flying in this house. It was so beautiful, so peaceful. This time, the intense light was in the center of the house, waiting for me. Or at least I thought it was waiting for me." She stopped. "I know it was. And I wasn't afraid. I went right up as close as I could to it. I walked into it, the light. It felt good and warm, and so comforting. I just...melted into it, and I felt something. I can't describe it, but I felt it. I know that something...profound happened to me."

"Mary, did you notice the man or woman in the light that you had seen before?"

"No. This time it was just the light. That uncommon, radiant light, drawing me into it. I remember flashing on the movie 'Field of Dreams.' I remember thinking, when I went into it, about the line that Kostner asks his father...something like, 'Is there a Heaven?' and then his father answers, 'Oh yea, it's the place where dreams come true.' And then the son, Kevin Kostner, says, 'Maybe this is Heaven.' I thought maybe I'd died in my sleep and this was Heaven. I just knew that I never, ever wanted to leave it. It was better than anything, pure bliss. I have been waiting for it to happen again, but I get the feeling that it never will. I want to know what it is, or was, and how to experience it again if I can. I won't rest until I find out."

Session Two

We made an appointment for three weeks later. I suggested that Mary journal her former dreams and any dreams that she might have in the future. It was a rainy Tuesday in May when she returned. She seemed much more at ease than she did in our last visit. I noticed that she wore the same hiking boots and the same white cotton sweater that she had worn in her last visit. She had on a pair of tan shorts. I greeted her with a hug. She was talking even before she sat down.

"He found my journal, about my dreams, and now he, Tony, my husband...remember? He thinks I'm a witch. He thinks I've gotten into something like a cult and my mind has been brainwashed. He thinks that is why I have all of these weird ideas about going back to school and teaching." She laughed. "He really had to dig deep to find it." She held up her notebook. "I'm surprised he did. He must go through everything. I'm really, really determined to get that divorce now. It's like I'm his prisoner. I've spoken to a lawyer already, and she says that she is worried about me, my safety. She's afraid that Tony will go off the deep end when I tell him. She had me memorize the address of a safe house. I didn't even know there was one here."

"Are you worried Mary?"

"No I'm not. I know Tony, and his family. He will obsess for maybe a month, and then he'll remarry within the year. Some other Stepford-type woman who will take care of him. And that's fine. I want him to be happy. I just can't be with him. He doesn't trust me because he thinks I have a life different than his. And he is right, more right than he knows. I'm just anxious to get going on my new life, where I actually have one." She laughs again. "It feels so good to be alive, even in the rain. I am really enjoying the spring!"

"So, Mary, what would you like to focus on today?" I ask.

"I would really like to find out...about the dreams and my experience with the light." She looked suddenly sad. "I have not had another dream or experience with that since our last session. But, that experience changed me. It...motivated me to do something worthwhile with my life. Can we somehow find out what that experience was?"

"Of course," I answered. "It's like St. Auxbury said in The Little Prince: 'What is essential is invisible to the eye.'"

During our hypnotherapy session, it was revealed that Mary had chosen for herself prior to her birth, a difficult childhood with her family because she had some sort of awareness to gain...She needed or wanted to experience how suffering such painful circumstances might feel. I directed Mary to go to the last time she had the experience with the light energy in her dream.

"Mary what is happening?" I asked.

"I'm walking toward it. I can't keep away."

"Mary, do you know who or what this light is?"

Her eyes fluttered. "It is the same Light that is reflected from within all of us."

"So the light was coming from you?"

She was silent for a few moments, and then she said to me, "It is that and more. It is the Higher Aspect of the birth soul, the Aspect that resides here within the body now."

I thought for a moment. "Is Mary, the Mary that was born

---

in the body, is she still there?" I asked.

"No, she has completed her work, her destiny. She has moved on." Mary's voice had gained intensity and directness.

"Who is here now? In this body?"

"I am her Higher Aspect."

"And where are you from?" I asked.

"The Seventh Plane...the place of teachers and masters."

"So is this Higher Aspect in the physical body that is still called Mary?"

"That is correct. It is what you might call the Higher Aspect of that same soul. The exchange was made nearly two months ago, in her sleep, as she told you and I now clarify for her mind's awareness and her emotional curiosity."

I was amazed at the detachment between the soul and the body that it inhabited, an almost clinical relationship, it seemed. "And what place was Mary from?"

"The Fourth Plane."

"When was this transfer arranged?"

"It was before the birth. Prior. It works well that way with those who have just a bit of karma to heal, to begin the physical life. But when the Higher Aspect merges with the body, the world service begins."

I wondered why Mary had had such a difficult childhood...I also wondered if this occupation by this energy that called itself the Higher Aspect was really serving the Highest Good for Mary or the world. I said, "If it is in Divine Order for us to do so, I would like to go to that time just before the birth to review that agreement. We will ascend seven steps to reach that plane of existence at the time just prior to your birth. One-two-three-going up to four-five-six, to seven. You are there now. Look around you. What do you sense, feel, or see?"

There was silence, and then, "Twelve, there are twelve called Planners here."

"On the table is the contract. Pick up the contract and read the agreement. All that you need to know is there. What is Higher Aspect's purpose in this body?"

"To teach, to heal, to assist others to find their way. To help with the Earth in the unfolding of Her destiny as well... concerning the consciousness of humanity.."

I could tell that she was reading from the `contract'. "Why have you come in at this particular time?"

"If people do not change, do not learn, there will be a cleansing of the Earth, yes, just as has been predicted. It has begun, and some of us entering in now are directing our own to safety. Those who are not responding to our messages." Her voice was kind and concerned. "It is necessary if things do not change. The cleansing is directly related to the consciousness or unconsciousness of humanity. It is necessary."

"Does Higher Aspect have a twin flame as we call it?"

"Yes. The name is Michael."

I knew of other "mergers" that occurred after the soul exchange, and asked, "what is the process or relationship of Higher Aspect and Michael?"

"They are integrated. They came in to the body that way, together, two parts of the same whole. That is the completeness of the Higher Aspects."

"And who or what was the man or woman figure that Mary saw

in the light in her dream?"

"Another from the Seventh Plane who was acting as a guide for her. He tried to communicate, but the vibrational frequency had not been properly callibrated. It was not possible."

"Is there anything that the body/mind of Mary needs to know at this time?"

"How to protect the Self from negative human activity until the active karma is complete; the karma that has already been set in motion. There are those who do not understand, who would use her positive energy for their own devices, as they are accustomed to in the past relationship. Those here will help."

"Her husband?"

"He is already sexually involved with another female at work, and the way will be easy now."

"Does Mary know? Did she know?"

"Now she does. But that does not matter. Only the drop of water shattering the stillness of the leaf."

"How many Walk-Ins are on the planet Earth at this time, like you, Higher Aspects of the Self, from the Seventh Plane?" I asked.

"There are one thousand six hundred and fifty-four."

"How many are there in total?"

Without hesitation she replied, "There are Higher Aspects for all of us from there. There has to be a catalytic event or a reaching upward, a change in consciousness as it it called, that creates the need or awareness of that existence."

"And what was that for Mary," I asked.

"It was the ever reaching upward in selfless prayer."

"Is there any special significance when the Higher Aspect changes places?"

"Yes, but one that is different for each aspiring soul. It greatly accelerates the progress of both aspects of the soul on the path of greater purpose." Mary's voice was a whisper.

Following our session, I asked Mary how she felt about her experience.

"I knew that something really different had happened about a couple of months ago. I've had the sense that I have been attending conferences or some kind of meetings during my sleep for about a year, but I never remember anything at all about it. I'd cry myself to sleep at night and yet wake up feeling better and better."

"Mary," I asked, "Do you remember what was said about Tony?"

Her eyes opened wider. "Yes! I do, I remember now! That's unbelievable, but believable at the same time. He keeps telling me I'm 'neglecting' him, if you know what I mean."

"How do you feel about the information?" I wondered if she felt betrayed.

"I think it really makes it easy for me now. I'll somehow let him know that I know. Or maybe he'll tell me before I get to that. It will all be my fault, but I'm way beyond any fear or blame that he might want me to feel responsible for. In a way I am so relieved. It's a freeing thought. In fact, I've never felt so free in my entire life! The Universe works in mysterious ways."

"So what will you do?" I asked.

"I have come to help our Earth children experience life as a spiritual journey, and to remember just how important they are. They can make a difference in the consciousness of this planet. But first..." she smiled at me, "First, I have to deal with some unfinished business."

I knew that she was referring to the playing out of active karma. Following that arrow shot from the bow of active karma by the hand of fate to its final resting place in the field of freedom's destiny.

Third Soul, Same Body

"I can't stand this pain anymore, I want to die. I want to just die!" Sharon's eyes shimmered with tears. "Dr. Reneau referred me to you. She said that you might be able to help. I've had every test. I spent my life's savings trying to find out what is wrong with me, with this body." She crossed her arms. "The formal diagnosis is Fibromyalgia. But this isn't just plain Fibro from what I've read. This body is trying to get back at me for something I've done to it, consciously or subconsciously. You could call it pay back or karma. I feel like I'm being tortured with every move that I make."

I had to reflect for a moment. It seemed to me that I get two types of referrals from medical doctors. One type of referral carries the label of terminal dis-ease; when they (the more sensitive doctors) want their patient to find counseling and comfort in the dying, or what I call the "transition" process. Most of these people are able to survive the curse of pending doom when they experience a change in consciousness through counseling. The second type of referral involves spiritual dis-ease that is at this time in our medical history, is physically immeasurable. Tests after tests are performed, and generally the patient is exposed to every possible drug attached to every minute symptom that they may report. I have come to regard both types of referral as a rare opportunity for spiritual growth. In Sharon's case, I had more to learn. I knew that, as always, I needed to step back and allow the Higher Self to reveal the root cause of her pain.

She continued, "Dr. Reneau said that you could help people when nothing else worked." She then related work that I had done previously with a colleague of Dr. Reneau's who worked in a clinic in New Jersey. "I've tried everything. Absolutely everything. She handed me a page of therapies that she had attempted and a list of prescription drugs and herbal therapies. "You see I've tried hypnosis. I can't be hypnotized."

I smiled at her. I have never encountered an individual in my ten years that would not work with me and attain an altered state of consciousness if they wanted to find healing. Generally a person who says that they cannot be hypnotized has a misunderstanding or misconception about what hypnotherapy actually is, or perhaps a deep seated fear of somehow losing control. Trust is important. "That isn't important to me, Sharon. I can work in my own field of what I call 'Higher Self Therapy.'"

"And I thought I'd heard of everything. So, what is it, how does it work?" She winced in pain as she sat back on the couch.

"I do a form of energy work called Reiki."

"I do Reiki! I love Reiki," she said. "It is the only thing that has helped me ease the pain in my shoulders."

I smiled at her. "Good. Then you know how powerful it can be. Reiki energy work allows us a spiritual access to the body, mind, and emotions that may otherwise be blocked. While I'm working on certain chakras, I ask simple questions that may or may not make sense to you. You answer them if you choose. It is a specialized technique of Reiki that I now teach to others. I call it "Transformational Reiki®." Following the session, the healing will continue. Sometimes it is like the twenty-one day healing or clearing process that occurs after each class in Reiki."

"So I'm on the Reiki table?"

"Yes, but only if you're comfortable there, Sharon."

"Most comfortable. Most comfortable."

Session One

I knew instinctively that I would probably only have one session with Sharon and that it would prove intense for both of us.

I began at her head, at the Crown Chakra. It felt to me as if someone had left a door open there, something had never experienced. I never relate what I personally feel to a client during a Reiki session, as I feel that that may alter their own healing potential. I am merely a channel.

"Sharon, I would like for you to take three deep breaths, and as you breathe in, breathe in blue, and as you exhale, relax and let go. Release all of your thoughts, all of your cares, all of your worries of the day." Her entire body began to tremble uncontrollably. *"Would you*

like a heavier blanket?"

"No." She whispered. "Nothing like this has ever happened to me before."

"Are you okay? Do you want me to go on? You are in control of everything, I would never force you to do anything that makes you uncomfortable." I said.

"I'm all right. Just surprised that this is happening. Something major is going to happen. I felt it the minute you put your hands on my head. It is most intense right here." She pressed her hand to the center of her chest. "I feel like someone is sitting on my heart."

"What does it look or feel like to you?"

"Dark. It's very dark. Like a huge dark cloud pushing down on me. I can hardly breathe."

I knew that we had to hurry. "Is this serving your Highest Good?"

"No. No. It scares me. This scares me."

"How long has it been with you?"

"I don't understand this. It left at twenty-one and wants back in. It says the body belongs to it." She suddenly starts to cry, sobbing violently.

"Are you ready to let it go?" I ask.

"I need to maybe talk to it first. To understand it."

"Then tell it to back off from your chest. It must stop pushing." Her breathing and panic eased. "Good. Now you can talk to it. Take your time. I also ask for Divine Protection and Guidance for you in this process." (Protection and guidance are an integral part of Reiki. I spoke the words aloud to comfort her.)

"Body Rights. It says it has Body Rights. Rights to my

body? But why?" She fell silent, listening, thinking, debating. "But you left the body for dead, remember? You abandoned it." Silence, and then: "But why don't you just go on?" She started to cry again. "So you've been doing this to me? Because you want this body back? You have no right!" She was angry now. Her body was tense and quivering. "Now she has my throat!" She grabbed both sides of her throat and pulled.

"Tell her she must stop or we will send her away now."

She relaxed. "She stopped. She is upset that I found you. She knows who you are. She seems to be afraid of you. She is really sad."

"Tell her she cannot harm you now in any way."

"She won't."

"How did this happen?" I ask.

"I had a car accident when I was twenty-one. They tell me I was clinically dead. They pronounced me dead at the scene. She left. She tells me I came in and took over. It took almost a year of physical therapy to even be able to walk."

"Did you have any pain after that?" I asked.

Her eyes opened. "For three years I suffered pain. But then it all gradually faded away. Except for some fuzziness in my joints."

"Close your eyes now, and keep contact with the other one." (I was hesitant to use the word 'soul.') "Why did it come back to this body?"

"To try to get it back. It is angry that I took over. The body was supposed to die. She had planned for the body to die."

"So why did you come in?" I asked.

"Because this one created a spiritual violation. I came to correct it."

"What is this other one's real name?"

"I don't know."

"Ask it what is your real name?"

"Sistoe. No. It is Susto. Susto means curse or negative energy."

"What did Susto do that was a spiritual violation?"

"It tricked the first soul out of the body."

"How did it do that?" I asked.

"Barter. It was like selling your soul or betting with the devil."

"Can that really happen?"

"It did with her. She wanted someone so badly. She loved him so much that she bargained with this Susto." She started to cry. The memory of that experience was a part of the body's Akasha.

"And what happened next?" She asked.

"She got him and then she found out he wasn't at all like he pretended to be. They say be careful what you ask for, you might get it. She really learned to hate him. He lied to her and cheated all the time. He violated her unmercifully. He beat her and stole her money and spent it on drugs and alcohol. What a sad lesson. Then the Susto took over the body. By that time she, the first Sharon, didn't care. She left without a fight. But she was tricked. The Susto made him do those awful things I think. It got in his ear and gave him bad ideas."

"Where is he now?"

"Married. Happily married with no substance abuse issues. The Susto did that."

"And where did you come from?" I asked.

"I was watching the whole thing from the Higher Astral Plane.

But I couldn't interfere until the Susto murdered the body. I couldn't let that happen. We do not like Sustos to win. It reflects badly upon the Light for the darkness to win so easily. So the Susto took this as a challenge to reclaim the body and has been attacking the Subtle and Etheric bodies to get even. Fraying the wires. If it were in the physical body, it would be considered Multiple Sclerosis. They thought at first it might be that; where the Myliten Sheath is frayed away in places. But no test can show it happening in bodies other than the physical."

"I want to speak directly to the Susto if that is okay with you Sharon."

"Okay."

"Susto, whatever damage you have created here, I now demand that you repair. I know you have the means to do this, and through the Power of Grace and the Law of Light, I demand and command that you repair all that you have done now. And I ask that someone from the Highest Light assist you in this process so that everything is repaired and restored to its optimum well being."

Sharon begins to shake her right arm, wrist, and hand. "She is working on my shoulders and arm on the right side. I can feel it." She sounds surprised.

For the next twenty minutes we work with energy and the repairs of the Susto. When we finish, I ask if there is anything else that the Susto needs to fix. Sharon asks the Susto, and it seems that the work is complete. I am curious, and ask why the Susto does such things.

The Susto replies: "It is what we do to assist people with their spiritual growth."

"But How?" I ask. "How could such a violation teach anyone anything?"

"One cannot learn about the Light unless they also experience darkness. It is what we do. We serve also. We serve as a contrast."

"Sharon, are you ready to let this one go?"

"Do you need to heal any feelings with this Susto?" She nods her head no. "Then I want you to open a door of Light and ask that this one be taken to its place of Highest Spiritual Development away from here. Just say the word 'go' three times, and release this Susto." Her back arches off the table, and when she relaxes, she seems peaceful. "Are you all right?"

"Yes." She whispers.

I count her back and she opens her eyes.

"Did you know all of this was going on before we started?" She asked.

"I knew that something was going on." I smiled at her. "I'm used to the unexpected. The more detached I am from desiring a particular outcome or thought, the more useful I am to you. So, how do you feel?"

"Strange. Very strange. Like there's a fire inside of me. Am I still sweating?" Her shirt was soaked with perspiration.

"No. I'm going to wrap you in this light blanket to prevent chills or a sudden energy shift." I get her a cup of room temperature water.

"You know what," she said. "I have always said that I feel like I am living in a hollow tree. That's the image I've always had. You know, like there's this irritable interface going on. Now it makes sense. If I'm the third soul in this body, it may be developing an allergic reaction. Like a chemical reaction."

It made sense to me. "Do you feel that it is possible to heal this reaction?"

"I'm going to really put my Reiki to work," she said. "And something else. I have really been studying, fascinated by Feng Shui. Do you know what that is? The Oriental Art of Placement. Wind and Water. Of course you do." She waved her hand around my office to the placement of certain objects and mirrors. "I need to Feng Shui my body. We just Feng Shuied the Spirit, now I'm going to Feng Shui the Body." She seemed much more at ease as she left my office. I never heard from Sharon again.

Icon Studio, Island of Santoria, Greece
Photo by Matthew Mitchell

Wisdom from the Buddha:

"The human mind discriminated itself from the things that appear to be outside itself without realising that it has first created these very things within its own mind. This has been going on since beginningless time and the delusion has become firmly fixed within the mind, and even adheres to the things themselves. Because of this discrimintation between the self and the not-self the mind has come to consider itself as an ego-personality and has become attached to it as being something different and more enduring than the things of the world. Thus, the people of the world grow up in ignorance of the fact that discrimination and thinking of ego-personality are nothing but activities of universal mind.

"Universal Mind, while remaining pure and tranquil and unconditioned in its self-nature, is the source of all mental processes and is, thus, the foundation for the other two minds and retains within itself all their experiences. The Mind, therefore, like a waterfall, never ceases its tumult of waves because of some passing tempest, so the ocean of the mind becomes stirred by tempests of delusion and winds of karma. And just as the ocean again becomes peaceful when the tempest passes, so the Ocean of Mind resumes its natural calm when the winds of karma and delusion are stilled...If people can change their view-points, can break up these age-old habits of thinking, can rid their minds of the desires and infatuations of egoism, then the wisdom of true enlightenment is possible."[4]

---

4. The Teaching of Buddha, by B.D.K., Kenkyusha Printing Co, Tokyo, Japan, 1966, pp. 48-50

From Thoreau's Walden:

"Morning is when I am awake and there is dawn in me."

"The millions are awake enough for physical labor; but only one in a million is awake enough for effective intellectual exertion, only one in a hundred million to a poetic or divine life. To be awake is to be alive."

"We must learn to reawaken and keep ourselves awake, not by mechanical aids, but by an infinite expectation of the dawn, which does not forsake us in our soundest sleep. I know of no more encouraging fact than the unquestionable ability of one to elevate the life be a conscious endeavor."

Henry David Thoreau, from Walden

Glastenbury Tor
Photo by Shauna Angel Blue

The Angelic Connection

> "If you'd known it was going to happen this way, would you have done it anyway?"
> "I would rather have had one breath of her hair, one touch of her hand...than an eternity without it. One."
>
> *From the motion picture: "City of Angels"*

"The baby is dying. The baby is turning blue. They can't do anything! They can't save the baby. But I can save the baby. I can save the baby..."

It was our second regression session. Elizabeth, recently engaged to be married, came to my office for help in understanding the root cause of the sudden onset of her life-threatening seizures. Her medical doctors were baffled. Her voice had changed at least a half an octave since we began. "Who can save the baby?" I asked.

"I have to. I have to! I have no choice, I'm going in, or the baby will die!" Then there was complete silence. I was not certain that Elizabeth was still breathing. I checked. She was softly breathing.

"Elizabeth, what's happening?" No answer. "Elizabeth," I repeated more loudly, "What's happening now?"

"She's going to be all right. The baby is going to be all right..her heart will heal. But I...I've lost my wings. My wings are gone! My friends are gone! Where are my wings? How long do I have to stay in here?"

Then Elizabeth was crying in sheer anguish. I tried to comfort her, but there was an overwhelming sense of despair and loneliness. I had asked that Elizabeth "Go back to the time the reason for her sei-zures exist," and we apparently had journeyed back to the time of her birth. "What is your name?" I asked.

"My name is...was...Lorra-El. I am called Elizabeth in this body."

"What do you mean your name was Lorra-El?"

"I was one of them, the Cherubim. Angels who communicate with humanity. We were having fun, playing our usual games, until I heard the mother cry. The mother of the baby. She knew the baby was going to die. They told her. The doctors told her. I don't know why I heard her, no one else seemed to hear her. Maybe God wanted me to hear her, wanted me to help. Or to see if I would. I just don't like being here. My last body was so much better...so comfortable and perfect in every way. I was attractive too. This body is not, it is so much trouble. It doesn't feel good. I don't like it. I don't like being her. I can't make this body do anything right."

"Elizabeth, what happened when you knew the baby was going to die?"

"I held my breath, and I went in. I had to."

"And then what happened?"

"She...the other one, the one that died, she flew off...she left. She was smart."

"And where did she go?"

"Where we all go. Back. Back to the One, the Golden Pool, the Infinite Pond."

"And you stayed?"

"I'm still stuck here. Without my wings. I miss my friends. It's so lonely here in this body. I don't like this body. I can't hear the others."

"Why did you stay, Elizabeth? And who was the one who left?"

"I had to stay for the mother. She is not the same as I am. She would have died. A part of her was dying. It was her last chance, there could be no more for her. It was all that she had."

"What do you mean by 'not the same as I'?"

"She, the mother, is not from the same group as we are. But it was her turn, the one who took off, she was in our group. It was not my turn. But I think I was offered the assignment to complete what she started. It was a challenge. We are challenged from time to time, just to keep in touch. For me, it has been over thirty years ago. I'd almost forgotten how it is to be in these human bodies. I've never had one like this before." Elizabeth started to cry again. "There's no way to fix this...I should have used better judgment." She was sobbing uncontrollably.

"Elizabeth," I said, "I want you to go just beyond this experience for now, and go to a place where we can gain more insight into what happened so we can heal whatever we need to heal or whatever we can heal, in Divine Order for the Highest Good, we are there now...Where are we Elizabeth?"

She became suddenly silent. "It's dusty. I hear horses running nearby. A man is yelling. He is being drug...by the horses. They almost trample me. I grab for the harness, but they keep running past me. The sleeve of my dress rips out. I can't stop them. I can't catch them. The man is dragging, caught behind them. I can't stop them!" She is hysterical, moving her head from side to side in the recliner.

"I want you to go just beyond this. I'm going to count from one to three, and you'll be just beyond this. One, two, three! I snap my fingers. Just beyond this, looking back, free of emotion." She breathes a sigh of relief and is quiet.

"He's dead you know." She whispers. "I couldn't save him. Couldn't stop them. There was this big rock."

"The horses, you tried to stop the horses?" I asked.

"Yes, the horses." She was tense but breathing normally.

"And who was the man?" I asked her.

"He was Charles. My husband. He survived the war. I really didn't think he would. I cried every night when I was alone. He was a farmer. I knew it was going to happen. I knew he would die before we could have children. I thought I could stop it. Could save him from what was planned. To give him a baby right away. That's what he wanted more than anything. But I'm not supposed to do that...to try to stop or change things. It gets me into trouble every time. I think I can save others...humans from their fate. From the death they may have chosen for themselves. Is this a punishment you wonder? No, not that. It is for me to gain a greater understanding. But I did decide to die after he did, and so I did. Less than a year. I just gave up. Can I heal this. Yes, of course. Will I? No, probably not. Not this time. I can't give up yet. Maybe next time. It's like a an addiction...or maybe a personal Tsunami. A Savior complex."

She was answering questions as they came into my thoughts. I did not have to verbalize my thoughts at all...I thought, "What is your name in that lifetime?"

"My name is Jesse. It is 1846. We live in West Virginia, near Charleston. I am a school teacher. I have loved Charles since I was twelve. We married when I was sixteen. He was twenty-two. We have no children yet. And won't." She started to cry again. "You don't understand the importance of his having a child. He was the last brother to survive the war. The other three did not. His parents were devastated. A baby was most important to them too, to continue the family bloodline. If you followed his family tree back, you would find his family to be one of the House of Sadoc that revolted against the majority. He was an ancient Essene. But the Essene bloodline is thinning. It is nearly extinct. What a loss to this planet when they are all gone."

I did not know what she meant by that, but knew that it was time to end the session. I gave her the suggestion that if it served the Highest Good, what she needed to know would come to her in dreams or in any other manner that was appropriate when she was ready to understand.

Session Three

This and following sessions have been condensed somewhat to include only vital information. Much of the hypnotic instruction between lifetimes has been removed.

Two weeks have passed. Elizabeth has Sam, her fiance, drive her to her appointment, as I have advised that she do so. As we chat, I learn that her seizures have not ceased but are less severe in intensity and shorter in duration. She has not been sleeping well at night. She believes that she is dreaming, but does not remember her dreams. We discuss our last session, and she admits that she does not remember much about what transpired during the session. I ask her how she would like to proceed with her therapy session today. She feels that our work has been beneficial, and that there is something going on that is deeper than her conscious mind will allow her to know. I know that her favorite color is green, and that her favorite peaceful place is the ocean. Soon she is relaxed, and we are once again in session. I asked her once again to go back to the time that the reason for her seizures exist.

"Everyone thinks that Angels are supposed to be perfect. Well, not all of them are. At least in my group we're not perfect. Oh, we try to be, but..." Elizabeth sighs deeply. "I should have let the baby die. But I couldn't let it happen. I kept thinking of Charles. His baby. The baby we never had because he died. I couldn't stop the death...his dying. So I tried to keep the baby alive." She started to sob quietly.

"Elizabeth." I said. "Are Angels supposed to keep people from dying?"

"No. we can't. Or at least I think we can't. I'm not sure. I tried to and it didn't work."

"What does Charles have to do with these seizures that Elizabeth is having?" I asked. She was quiet and did not answer. So I proceeded with another related question: "What do Charles and the baby have to do with Elizabeth's seizures?" Still no answer. Elizabeth was breathing as if she was asleep. "Elizabeth, do you hear me?"

"Yes, I hear you." She responded quietly. "I'm not certain that I, Lorra-El would have jumped into this defective body if it had not been for Charles. For that reason, birth seemed to be very important to me. So I was...too eager. I felt what the mother was feeling. I couldn't stand it. It was like watching Charles die all over again. I thought I was past all of that. We tend to forget, thankfully. But it came right back. We just pick up the buckets from the same place that we left them last time. There is a veil, but for some of us it is thinner than for others. The veil is thinning again, in this body, so the seizures have started."

"Elizabeth, what do you mean?"

"I know who I am, and who I was."

"You mean that you knew that you were Jesse?"

"No, that I was an Essene."

I remembered her reference to Charles in the last session as an "Essene". "So did you know Charles when he was an Essene?" I asked.

"Yes." She smiled. "He was then the soul of Josie, my teacher. The Righteous Teacher." She spoke reverently, but began to ramble. "She was an ancient woman, very old but young-looking, attractive. Yet she was so old we never knew. Some say that Josie was born to a dying baby's body in Atlantis... fully conscious, fully awake. Like the Hindu God they called Krishna. I loved Josie more than anyone else in Qumran. We all did. One day she just disappeared without a trace. She was persecuted constantly by the Maccabean high priests. God had revealed the Truth Far Beyond the Prophets to Josie. She told us how we the 144,000 came to this planet in a great spiral of Light; how we, the souls of our people, choose to walk-in upon wounded bodies and broken souls to recycle flesh and assist the human inhabitants. We often choose to be celebate as two of our souls in braided union of wholeness can inhabit one single body in complete bliss and harmony. We are celebate in Qumram as it serves our spiritual purpose of enriching this braided union. We grieved for years for Our Righteous Teacher. We could not find her soul! Some say that the Wicked Priest of Hasmonean ordered her murder and extinction. It is possible to extinguish a soul just as one can extinguish a candle's flame. That group of Maccabean's feared our power and spiritual strength. We never knew what they might have elected to do to Josie. I died not knowing her soul again." Tears were falling down her cheeks.

"What year did you die?" I asked.

"I died fifty years before Herod the Great was even conceived. Before the Great Prophet was born. Our method of keeping time was different then for us, but it was about 100 B.C. by your way of time."

"Did you ever meet the soul of Josie again?" I asked.

I met her again in Bath, and then we moved on from that spiritual gathering in search of our Qumran group. We went to Rennes-Le-Chateau in France. When we found the others, we became what history calls an obscure group of 'Cathars.' Religious zealots, martyrs. Josie was our Spiritual leader. I think she was the very same person, maybe even the same body. She remembered my soul and the soul of everyone in our group, her devout followers. There were over 4,000 of us, original souls gathered from Qumran there. And others. We died together; we were murdered, because we failed the order, the patriarchal edict of the Church. We were slaughtered by Simon de Montfort and his crusaders from the King of France." She was silent for some time.

"And what happened next?" I asked her.

"And then she became Charles. He waited for me to be born to flesh, to assume the body of Jesse, and then to grow up. But I failed him. I failed to conceive, failed to bring forth the life that he wanted. His baby." She started to cry once again. "I always let Josie down, I failed again with my mission."

"What do you mean, 'Always let Josie down'?"

"Every time we were together. In Qumran. If I had been a more serious student. In France, if I had only tried harder to convince her to give up the Sacred Cloth, to yield to the priests of the Church. And then, if only I could have conceived when she was with the body of Charles. Whenever I assume a body, I fail my mission." She stopped speaking abruptly.

"But what of free will? What about Josie's choices? How could you know she was going to be murdered in Qumran or France?" I asked.

"We knew something might happen. She knew very well what was going to happen. She always had the gift of Wisdom. And yet she just let it happen. She could have abandoned us, like she disappeared without a trace in Qumran."

"And in Qumran? Did you know that She was planning to leave?"

"No. She just vanished. I knew when I met her again in Bath...England, that she must just have abandoned us all."

"How was any of that your fault?" I asked. She remained silent. "Do you need to forgive yourself for these feelings that you have?"

"I can't forgive myself."

"Why not?" I asked.

"I just can't. That's all, I can't!" She started to cry softly.

I glanced at the clock and realized that it was time for our session to end. I gave her three post-hypnotic suggestions that we had agreed upon prior to this session, and asked that she remember everything and allow more to come to her at the appropriate time. When I brought her back, she wiped the tears from her eyes and sat up slowly. "How do you feel?" I asked.

"Sad. I am so sad. I know there is something else...there. Maybe we can get to it next time. Next week?" We confirmed the appointment and she left.

I felt that she was right, that we had not yet uncovered the root cause of her seizures. Sometimes the conscious mind protects even the subconscious mind from releasing Akashic Records that might be too painful for the individual to handle. Edgar Cayce often spoke of the Akashic Records, the repository of all information regarding an individual's past-lives. In one of his channelings, I remember that he said, "Every Soul shall give account of the deeds done in the body. What body? That body of mind, that body of physical manifestation, that body of spirit; each in its own sphere, its own realm." I believe he was referring to karma. There is a reference in Hinduism to three types of karma: active, dormant, and potential karma. Active karma is said to be similar to an arrow already shot from the bow. One must deal with where it lands, as there is no stopping its action. One has more choice with dormant and potential karma, as they are like the arrow in the quiver waiting to be shot forth from the bow, and the arrows yet to be created. I feel that past-life karma is active karma, and most people, and Walk-Ins in particular, must first clear the active karma before healing the past can clear the way for a more spiritual future. If the past is not healed, an individual is most likely to select an arrow from the quiver of dormant karma and shoot it off the bow at an unsuspecting world in a state of ignorant unconsciousness. As the saying goes, if we do not learn from our past mistakes, we are destined to repeat them. In Past-Life Regression Therapy, we call a mistake that is repeated lifetime after lifetime a "pattern". It is as if you are walking along enjoying life, when suddenly you fall into a deep hole and die. In the next three lifetimes, the same thing happens. In your fourth lifetime, you notice the hole, fall into it anyway and perish. In your fifth lifetime, you notice the hole, but this time you walk around it. You have healed the pattern by raising your consciousness in lifetime after lifetime through experience. Such lessons continue until there are no other patterns to heal. Enlightenment!

Session 4

"I think I have it figured out." Elizabeth greets me with a smile and a quick hug and throws her coat on the chair. There is something with Josie. That has to be it.

"And what makes you think that?" I smile back at her, reaching for my notes.

"Every time I think about her, even the name, I get really sad, and then I get angry. I think that thinking about her caused a minor seizure a couple of days ago. I was telling one of my friends about it, and the next thing I knew she was slapping my face and yelling at me."

"How have your seizures been, Elizabeth?"

"Just that one. That's all this week. That's progress."

We continued to talk about the events of her week for the next thirty minutes. Elizabeth was quite a gregarious individual. I asked her if she was ready to continue our work where we left off. She wanted to learn more about her relationship with her spiritual leader of two lifetimes, Josie. I directed her back to the most important event as it relates to her present life, that she shared with the soul named Josie.

"*Where are you?*" *I ask.*

"*France. Rennes-Le-Chateau. The year is 1208. On the hillside. We are walking on the hillside together in our robes. She is telling me that our lives will soon change. She has visions and knows these things. She is telling me that she wants me to know that she understands what I must do, that she forgives me what I am about to do.*"

"*What are you going to do?*" *I ask her.*

"*I don't know what she is talking about. Really I don't. I tell her that. She says I must remember what she has said. She has great power. She knows the Word. I know that we are always safe because she knows the True Word. We call her Mother Catharine.*"

She calls me Sister Jenife. I came into this body when it was seven, sickly and dying. It was a miracle at Lourdes they say. We have a simple quiet life, in sacred celebacy, all of us souls reunited from the village of Qumran. But then the priests from the church come. Women are not to lead in prayer, they say. It is heresy. All those who do will be punished, put to death. She continues to lead us in common prayer. I am furious with Catharine...that she will not stop even though she knows they might kill her. A part of me remembers Qumran and what happened there with the wicked priests. It's the same thing again. She is not learning from her mistakes. She is not listening to me." She became suddenly silent, tears were flowing from the corners of her eyes.

"And what happens next Jenife?"

"I told them. I told the men, the earlier crusaders with the priests who came here." She whispered. "I was so angry with her. I told them she wouldn't stop leading in prayer. Women are not to do such things anymore. It is forbidden by the Church. Heresy. The Pope and the King of France will no longer allow it. No more women priests...priestesses. I am afraid for all of us, I am a holy priestess too, so I told them. I told them!" She tossed her head from side to side. "I never imagined what they would do. That they could be so cruel. And I had to witness every minute of it. Catharine died a horrible, painful death. They burned her slowly, barbecued her from her feet, slowly up to her head. It was so painful for her! It was the worst way to die." She started to cry. "I could hear her pitiful screams, her agony, and then her crying out for forgiveness for them. And for me! She actually smiled at me and told me that she loved me, told me not to worry, when they took her away. I need to be punished.

Everyone was slaughtered because of me. We were buried in three mass graves, bodies stacked six to eight deep. I am punishing myself now. Slowly. Just like her death. From the feet to the head. That is the way the seizures move. From the feet to the head. If only I can bear her pain, that agony, little by little...maybe this sin will go away. We women who were priestesses were all slaughtered. We heretic women were to be the example for the rest of the Christian world. but what of the Innocents who were there? The others? The children? An example! To the lowly women who thought God might listen to them..." She was becoming hysterical. "And it happened again in Germany. Our next lifetime...we were all burned in the inquisition...the Black Sabbath. All of the women of our village were burned. The Church Fathers wanted to eliminate our religion. We were the Living Religion! The Religion of Life, not death, hell, and sin. But they could not control us and we refused to convert. Convert or die? There was no real choice. They feared us, they condemned us, and then they burned us. Wiped out the roots of our Living Tree...our religion. It happened again!" She stared to cry. "We never hurt them. Why?! Why did they do this?" She was turning her head from side to side, tears streaming down her cheeks. She was reliving the agony of the experience. This is not a necessary part of Past-life Regression Therapy.

I decided to move her out of the pain of this experience. "I want you to go just beyond this, breathing normally, move just beyond this experience now. Easily and effortlessly you move just beyond this." She relaxed and I handed her a tissue for her tears. She used it mechanically, still in a deep state of Alpha. Then I waited. "Good. Feeling better and better now. Take a deep breath and release any residue of pain that you might be holding onto. Now, looking back, at this experience, feeling safe and warm and protected, I want to know, how can you heal this?"

"I have to be punished." She blurted this out vengefully. "I am punishing myself now. I arranged this. In this body, I can punish myself. I betrayed her in Germany too. She taught me about the sacred plants..she saved me and I betrayed her. I told them she was a witch. I loved her and I betrayed her there too!"

"Jenife, Can't you forgive yourself for what happened instead of punishing yourself?" I asked.

"No, I can't forgive myself. I have no right to do that. God needs to forgive me! Catharine needs to forgive me! After all, I turned her in to them, to the Church fathers, to be tried and burned. I was the one who betrayed her. But she abandoned me in Qumran, left me, and I was in love with her. Truly in love with her. I held that against her. When she wouldn't stop, I betrayed her to get even. And she knew it! She said she forgave me before it even happened. But how could she forgive me? And all of the Innocents who died because of me?! I had no right to be what I was, to be a Cherubim, after that. I needed to burn. I needed to be punished, not to become someone's guardian angel. I just sort of took over...pushed her out of the way and took over her broken body so I could punish myself in the body."

"Jenife, I want you to go just beyond this memory, remembering everything, detached from the pain. One, two, three! You are just beyond this." She relaxed.

In a few moments I continued: "Why did you say you chose to come into this body?"

Tears were streaming down her cheeks. She answered quietly. "I said to punish myself. I knew I could make it happen in this body; I knew I could provoke it to punish me." Her voice changed. I knew she was no longer in France.

"Have you been punished enough yet?" I asked.

"No! Not yet. God has not spoken to me since that time. I was told that God would not listen to women, so I became deaf to the voice of God. Even as an Angel. Especially as an Angel. The next step is to fall, to completely let go of what we are and fall. Lose our Goldenness."

"If you became deaf to God's voice, did you choose that, or did God choose that?" I asked her.

She was silent for some time. "I believe I just shut the ears of my heart. Maybe I believed what the priests said, that God does not hear women. Or maybe I was afraid of the power of death. Maybe I was not good enough or worthy to hear what the others might hear. I was punishing myself. Like fasting. Only I, Lorra-El forgot to listen too, for the voice of God."

"How can you heal this?" I asked.

"Time. I need time. And the Grace and Word of God...Goddess...All That Is and Will Be." She sighed and then whispered a short, forgotten Essene prayer:

> "One may heal with goodness (God-ness)
> One may heal with justice,
> One may heal with herbs,
> One may heal with the Wise Word.
> Among all the remedies,
> This one is the healing one.
> That heals with the Wise Word."

Session Five

"I was trying on my wedding dress, and the next thing I know, I'm lying on the floor and my mother is holding my head, patting my cheeks, crying and yelling at me at the same time, like I'm a three year old trying to embarrass her." Elizabeth laughed. "It was worth it just to see the expression on her face. It was like all of the years when she wanted me to be like all of the other little girls and I wasn't. I believe she was angry with me for passing out on her in that swank bridal salon."

"So did you get the dress?" I teased.

"No. It made me look like a cow. Maybe that's why I passed out." She laughed again.

I was always amazed at Elizabeth's passionate, joyful response to life inspite of what was happening to her. "Was that your only seizure?" I asked.

"No, I had one at the mall, with Sam and our friends. We were just getting ready to go to a movie...Sam said that I all I had to do was tell him I really didn't want to go. He's pretty easy going, but this seizure rocked him a little. He was afraid I might die on him. He threw me into the car and off we went to the emergency room. He just left our friends stranded at the mall. I don't think they went to the movie either. They caught a ride home."

"I think we still need to look a little deeper at what is happening in your present life. Are you certain that you want to get married?"

She looked at me, surprised. "As certain as I am of anything. Unless..." She thought for a moment. "Unless there might be something subconscious. Should we check it out?"

"It seems that we are finding lots of different pieces to this puzzle of yours. Shall we get started?"

I had instructed Elizabeth to go to the time that the reason for her seizures exist. She began in France, and then quite suddenly, she flipped into another lifetime, like one domino falling upon another.

"I want you to look down at your feet. Tell me what you're wearing on your feet." I instructed.

"Boots. Black boots...just above the ankle. Black socks. Black dress. Everything black." She sighs.

"You have a coin in your hand, what is the date, the year on the coin?" I asked.

"I don't have any money. Right now I'm not allowed. But I do know the year. It's 1902. I'm seventeen."

"Look around you. Where are you?" I ask.

"Dubuque, Iowa. I'm on a hill overlooking a River. The Mississippi."

"Are you alone, or with someone?"

"Alone. No. There are other people. Women. Sisters."

"Your sisters?" I ask.

"No, nuns. I am with the Sisters of the Presentation. Not far from the Mother House. My name is Theresa."

"And Theresa, what are you doing?"

"I'm afraid to tell them I'm not sure that this is what I want to do." I will take my vows next month. I will teach elementary school. Until I get old and retire back to the Mother House. My whole life is planned for me. I never had a choice."

"What do you mean?" I ask.

"My father. We were from a big family. I am the oldest of nine...eleven. Two babies died right after they were born. My father told me I was to do this. As early as I can remember he was planning to send me off to the convent. And the others too. Except Andrew and John. They help him on the farm outside Dyersville. They are useful to him."

"And how do you feel about that, Theresa?"

"It's just the way things are when you don't have enough money to take care of everybody. It doesn't do any good to feel one way or the other. At least this way I get an education."

"Why are you having doubts?"

"Because I always dreamed of having my own family. A baby to hold. A baby." She starts to cry softly. "But I never will if I do this. I'll just have other people's children to care for, to teach."

"Theresa, go to the next most important event. What we need to look at."

"I go through with it. I am now the 'Bride of Christ'. The childless Bride of Christ. Barren again." She bites her lip.

"Does this event have anything to do in the future with the seizures of Elizabeth?"

She seemed to reflect for a moment and answered, "Yes."

"What?"

"The vows. Poverty. Chastity. Obedience to the Church. Forever, I believe."

"Forever?" I always caution people about the flagrant use of that word, as energy always follows intent. Forever, I say, is a long time. "Theresa, did you make an inappropriate vow or covenant that is now affecting the life of Elizabeth? Is her life now bound by that vow that you, Theresa, made then?"

"Yes it is. She cannot marry, ever. That would be adultery. We are wed to Christ. She cannot have children from any union."

"Is it fair to allow your decision at that time to affect her life now? Do you want her to be alone for the rest of her life?"

"No! I hated my life. I felt like I was a prisoner. I never spoke to my father again. No. I don't wish that life for anyone who doesn't willingly wish to serve in that way."

"Theresa, see, sense, or feel that your vows of poverty, chastity, and obedience are contained in a sacred scroll. You must hand this scroll to Elizabeth to decide if it serves her Highest Good to maintain them. Have you done this?"

Elizabeth holds out her hand as if receiving the scroll. "Yes, I have it."

"Review the contents of that scroll, of those vows, and decide if you wish to maintain them."

"No, I don't want to. Even as Essenes we could choose to marry. It was our choice. There were no vows. I want to marry Sam. I want a baby of my own." Tears are running down her cheeks.

"Then you must together burn that scroll and release yourself from those vows and covenents that no longer serve your Highest Good. Let me know when they are burned and you are completely free."

"Okay, they are just ashes now."

"Is there anything else that Theresa or you need to heal before you come back?"

"Yes, she really suffered. But she tells me the suffering was her choice. She tells me that yes, there are two kinds of suffering. One is inevitable suffering and the other is optional suffering. She wants me to avoid optional suffering. It doesn't do any good. I tell her I don't know what she means. She says that my seizures are optional suffering. I understand. My soul understands. I give her a hug. We are both feeling better. She just keeps getting lighter...she vanishes into thin air, she disappears. Now I see her grave marker in the convent cemetary. 1885-1938. I'm dropping the ashes of the scroll on her grave. I feel very sad for her. At least I have choices."

Session Six

It has been nearly a month since our last session, due to holidays and a typical Illinois winter snowstorm. I notice that she is walking with more ease and seems happier than I remember her from the past few sessions. She is carrying a small book with her.

"I know that you had mentioned before that I might read a book by Pema Chodron called, When Things Fall Apart. But I couldn't find it. But I did find this one." She smiled and handed me the pocket classic called Awakening Loving-Kindness by Pema Chodron. "Have you read this one? It is great." She took off her heavy tweed coat and scarf and sat down. "Look at the pages I have marked. They were perfect for me. Just what I needed." She pointed to the dog-earred pages from sixty-five to sixty seven. I began to read:

"There's another story that you may have read that has to do with what we call heaven and hell, life and death, good and bad. It's a story about how those things don't really exist except as a creation of our own minds. It goes like this: A big burly samurai comes to the wise man and says, 'Tell me the nature of heaven and hell.' And the roshi looks him in the face and says" "Why should I tell a scruffy, disgusting, miserable slob like you?" The samurai starts to get purple in the face, his hair starts to stand up, but the roshi won't stop, he keeps saying, "A miserable worm like you, do you think I should tell you anything?" Consumed by rage, the samurai draws his sword, and he's just about to cut off the head of the roshi. Then the roshi says, "That's hell." The samurai, who is in fact a sensitive person, instantly gets it, that he just created his own hell; he was deep in hell. It was black and hot, filled with hatred, self-protection, anger, and resentment, so much so that he was going to kill this man. Tears fill his eyes and he starts to cry and he puts his palms together and the roshi says, "That's heaven."

"There isn't any hell or heaven except for how we relate to our world. Hell is just resistance to life. When you want to say no to the situation you're in, it's fine to say no, but when you build up a big case to the point where you're so convinced that you would draw your sword and cut off someone's head, that kind of resistance to life is hell.

"In the way we practice, we don't say, "Hell is bad and heaven is good" or "Get rid of hell and just seek heaven," but we encourage ourselves to develop an open heart and an open mind to heaven, to hell, and to everything. Why? Because only then can we realize that no matter what comes along, we're always standing at the center of the world in the middle of sacred space, and everything that comes into that circle and exists with us there has come to teach us what we need to know.

"Life's work is to wake up, to let the things that enter into the circle wake you up rather than put you to sleep. The only way to do this is to open, to be curious, and develop some sense of sympathy for everything that comes along, to get to know its nature and let it teach you what it will. It's going to stick around until you learn your lesson, at any rate. You can leave you marriage, you can quit your job, you can only go where people are going to praise you, you can manipulate your world until you're blue in the face to try to make it always smooth, but the same old demons will always come up until finally you have learned your lesson, the lesson they came to teach you. Then those same demons will appear as friendly, warmhearted companions on the path."[5]

She was waiting patiently for my reaction. "Don't you get it? I'm the samurai! I've been creating my own hell all of these years, all of those lifetimes. Catharine was the roshi, the teacher. Her patience! And in this life, maybe, just maybe, I've been creating my seizures to punish myself for creating that hell. That was what Theresa meant by my 'optional suffering.' Doesn't it make sense to you?"

"Of course it makes sense to me, Elizabeth. But the question is, what are you going to do now that you believe this is true?"

She smiled at me. "That's the point." She was demonstrating with her hands. "If I have the power to create heaven or to create hell...from now on, I'm just going to create heaven. I'm sure that God knew I'd get there eventually. And Josie knew it too. That's why she didn't stop me. Why she forgave me. Why she forgave them. I think she was merely playing a role to help us to learn...to help us with our lessons. She was such a great teacher. The teacher of the Teacher.

5. Pema Chodron, Awakening Loving-Kindness, Shambhala Publications, Boston, Mass,. 1991, pp. 65-68

She taught us all about heaven. And then some of us went out and created our own hell. We had to learn. We just chose to learn the hard way. But we learned just the same. That's all that matters. She taught us how to love. That love is the most important thing about life. I thought I took this body to keep the mother from suffering. But I realize that I needed to learn more about love. Life and Love are eternal."

And so they are...

Follow-up: Sam and Elizabeth were married in 1997 and are unable to have children.

Fountain at Bath
Photo by Shauna Angel Blue

From 20th C. Yiddish, by David Glatstein

See how whole it all is,
not dimished for a second,
how you age with the days
that keep dawning,
how you bring your lived-out day
as a gift to eternity.

Monestary of John of Patmos, Patmos, Greece
Photo by Matthew Mitchell

On-Line Interview With A Walk-In

KM: What has your life been like? For example, has it been at all different than the childhood experiences of others, or have you ever considered yourself to be different in any way?

WI: I have always been different. I respond differently and react with an intense energy which admittedly has gotten me down some unusual paths. I must say, not all good ones. I love to discover and I love Truth. One time I asked my dad if he remembered any time when he could say I was different. I was looking for his view of the body around the walk-in time. It didn't take him long to answer, "No, I can't say I noticed anything out of the ordinary; you have always been different. Always off in a corner by yourself. Always alone. Always doing something unusual. I was blessed with a great mother and father. They always explained things to me and always sincerely encouraged the spirit of growth within me. I still remember my dad reading to me and explaining and explaining things to me. He never once complained that I was asking too many questions. And I was full of them. He never got tired of this; his role on my Path. My mother was dedicated to love. She was gentle, kind, and always giving. She gave out of what she never had. My mom left the Earth Plane at a young age of fifty-nine. It was her heart that took her. The heart that gave and gave and finally said, "I am tired and want to go home." My parents gave me the love they never had. They allowed me to be me; as unusual as that was. I always loved nature. I loved to listen to the wind and to watch the trees move. I loved the faces and shapes I saw in the clouds. It was fascinating to watch the winged ones. I discovered that healing took place as I lay on Mother Earth. I could hear the waters sing praises of life itself. Mother Earth and the animals were my very best friends. I guess you could say that they were my only friends. My guard was always up. I never let anyone inside for I soon learned that no one understood me. I really believe that if you want to get close to God you must first be close to animals. I really do.

I created a lot of my own pain. I was married to an abusive alcoholic for twenty years. Emotional pain almost destroyed me and I almost destroyed my children by my detachment from my emotions. But I always knew there was a reason for these trials. I learned patience and trust from the very depths of despair where I allowed my emotions to bring me. I finally realized that my lower ego was keeping me from the very Sacred Source I so earnestly longed for. When I said, "nevertheless not my will, but Thine be done," I meant it. Jesus and the Precious Holy Spirit brought me from the deepest pit of depression imaginable literally in an instant. All depression left and the desire for any drinking completely vanished. I was truly filled with peace. A nervous breakdown was replaced with deep inner joy and a peace not of this world.

KM: How long have you been aware that you are a Walk-In?

WI: Formally about seven years now.

KM: Are you aware of how and when the soul exchange occurred?

WI: The human body was born August 10, 1943 at 6:43 a.m., and my soul entry took place July 3, 1953 at 3:04 p.m. I can see my body on the ground by a fence. I don't know if it was a literal fence or just stating the end of this path. I would have been ten years old. I was also above and watching the process. I saw a very large entity bringing my soul and taking back the soul that was presently occupying the body. This entity/vessel of the Light came on a literal dimensional track. Almost like one rail of a railroad track. It was of a large oval form and had a huge smile. It was a very strong entity and one of Divine Protection and Intent.

KM: Why do you feel that the soul exchange took place? Was there a prior agreement of some sort?

WI: The soul exchange had to take place. We are a Dedicated Twin Flame in Sacred Service. We have consistently traded places since the beginning of Creation. This allows for the balance of the Path. Depending on Divine Purpose for a particular Earth Path, one of us is born first to lay the foundation of male or female energy patterns. I am female this time, and my Twin Flame came in first as a male. When I was in grade school, I was sometimes taken for a boy and was much more comfortable climbing trees and such. My last lifetime I was a male. This helps to balance the Flame.

I cannot say that we had a prior agreement because we already are One. Our Path just is. An agreement is not a consideration for us. The heart of this particular Flame has already been purged and tested eons ago. Our heart is one with Divine Purpose.

KM: Is there a reason that you feel you have come to the Earth at this time?

WI: To fulfill my part in the Destiny of the Divine Plan.

KM: How has your life changed since you became aware that you were a Walk-In?

WI: My life has not changed, for my search of who I am and what I came for has always been one of the deepest energy commitment. What it did do is confirm my feelings that I did come from the Stars. That felt really good. I feel that those who are Walk-Ins and those that are not have the same paths and goals as anyone else. The path of an Earthling might be a little different, but the footsteps are still taken one at a time. No path is better, no path is smarter, no path is greater--just different. We are truly all parts of each other. We need each other. The same metaphysical laws apply whether you are an extraterrestrial or terrestrial. Angel or other. Walk-In or not. Do not get hung up on emotions and/or judging. Allow the Divine and Sacred Angels of Mercy, Grace, and Compassion to assist in the healing and manifestation of your Highest Path.

KM: What is your purpose now? Your future goals? What do you feel is the future of the Earth?

WI: My purpose is committed to be of Divine Service in healing and teaching and to allow the Vessel of my heart to the the earth home for the Light of God. The answer is so simple. Truly love God first and your neighbor as yourself. Period. Compassion. Compassion. Compassion.

My goals are to continue to expand the High Heart and live in Divine Compassion releasing the self-judgment that has been most difficult for me to over-come. Spirit communicated to me that judging is sticky energy and that sure is true. I feel the future of the Earth is truly in our hands and that we have only a short time to make a difference. Divine compassion is the key. Keep your path clear and always look behind you. What kind of an energy path are you leaving? Don't add to the karma already here. Transmute it. Earth and the truly innocent life forms are set for almost complete destruction if humankind does not wake up and start walking the Path of Divine Love.

Keep your focus and remember that many of your experiences are just holograms. They are not truly real. You just think they are. There are energies of lesser light trying to destroy the discovery of the Joy of walking your Highest Path. Make a choice for integrity in your daily walk. You can transmute this lesser light by using Divine Love and Compassion. Meditate and pray and send love around the world. Remember nothing is impossible, we can make a difference.

There is truly a New Earth in our Creator's Plan. It is a very High Energy Sacred Entity. It is a very beautiful place. The transmutation has already begun, so let us prevent any further extinction of Divine life forms. We must move quickly or our beautiful animals will not be with us when the Dimensional Transmutation is complete. The animals have much to teach us. They are our Elders.

Learn of Sirius for she is a key player in the Universe at this time. Meditate regularly with her. Open your heart to her for she is waiting to teach us our next steps. If you walk out on the darkest night, you will see her radiant beauty. One great light in the darkness. That is Sirius, and that is you and me. One light truly can make a difference.

Well, Dr. Mitchell, there is part of my story. Thank you for asking. I hope some have related and found answers; and some have found their own Joy of Service as I have. I highly regard your own work on the earth plane at this time. Your Path and your work has been a real Blessing to me. And from my Heart to your Heart, I thank you for being my friend, and one whom I am Honored to Serve with.

I send you Joy. Humbly, I am your Essene friend.

The Angel of Life

"Seek not the law in thy scriptures, for the law is
   Life,
Whereas the scriptures are only words...
In everything that is life the law is written.
It is found in the grass, in the trees,
In the river, in the mountains, in the birds of heaven,
In the forest creatures and the fishes of the sea;
But it is found chiefly in thyselves.
All living things are nearer to God
Than the scriptures which are without life.
God so made life and all living things...
God wrote not the law in the pages of books,
But in thy heart and in thy spirit.
They are in thy breath, thy blood, thy bone;
In thy flesh, thine eyes, thine ears,
And in every little part of thy body. (p.35)[6]

---

6. The Essene Gospel of Peace Book Three, Lost Scrolls of the Essene Brotherhood, by Edmond Szekely, page 35

From: <u>Pale Blue Dot</u>, by Carl Sagan

"We lack consensus about our place in the Universe. There is not generally agreed upon long-term vision of the goal of our species--other than, perhaps, simple survival. Especially when times are hard, we become desperate for encouragement, unreceptive to the litany of great demolitions and dashed hopes, and much more willing to hear that we're special, never mind if the evidence is paper-thin. If it takes a little myth and ritual to get us through a night that seems endless, who among us cannot sympathize and understand?

"But if our objective is deep knowledge rather than shallow reassurance, the gains from this new perspective far outweigh the losses. Once we overcome our fear of being tiny, we find ourselves on the threshold of a vast and awesome Universe that utterly dwarfs--in time, in space, and in potential--the tidy anthropocentric proscenium of our ancestors...Despite determined resistance in every age, it is very much to our credit that we have allowed ourselves to follow the evidence, to draw conclusions that at first seem daunting: a Universe so much larger and older than our personal and historical experience is dwarfed and humbled, a Universe in which humanity, newly arrived, clings to an obscure clod of matter..."

The significance of our lives and our fragile planet is then determined only by our own wisdom and courage. We are the custodians of life's meaning. We long for a Parent to care for us, to forgive us our errors, to save us from our childish mistakes. But knowledge is preferable to ignorance. Better by far to embrace the hard truth than a reassuring fable.

If we crave some cosmic purpose, then let us find ourselves a worthy goal." (p. 51-55)

"I believe it is healthy--indeed essential--to keep our frailty and fallibility firmly in mind. I worry about people who aspire to be 'god-like.' But as for a long-term goal and sacred project, there is one before us. On it the very survival of our own species depends. If we have been locked and bolted into a prison of the self, here is an escape hatch--something worthy, something vastly larger than ourselves, a crucial act on behalf of humanity..." (p.333)

There is a mission. There is always a mission. However, the nature and essence of that mission is rarely revealed until the soul's light has been properly calibrated to fit the essence of Earth Energies. And then the Walk-in awakens to the dawn of a new world, a new purpose, a new Light...Seek always the Light, and may that Light shine in you as well.

Namaste,

The Light in me reaches out to the Light in you...

Karyn K. Mitchell, 1999

In GRATITUDE

I thank you for choosing this book and reading it, for in doing so, we have walked a path together, a rather intimate journey through time and space and even other dimensions. I would never ask you to embrace my Truth, for you have your own which defines you as the Light you are. If you have enjoyed the journey, please share this book with one other person.

I also wish to share my gratitude with Steven Mitchell and Bob Tentinger, for their patience; artists/photographer Shauna Angel Blue and Willie Koehler; Photographer and loving son Matthew Mitchell; and the kind words by writer Tami Gramont.

The Holy Bible states that "We see through the glass but darkly, if at all." I wonder if that is a conscious choice that we make from lifetime to lifetime, or if that is part of a greater plan for the evolution of humanity. In Buddhism, we learn that if we wish to understand our past lives, all we have to do is look deeply at our present condition. If we wish to know the condition of our future life, all we have to do is observe our actions today. There is a saying by a Great Teacher, "Tomorrow or the next life, which comes first?"

Give yourself permission to make this life what you want it to be. This is not a practice. I have heard too many people say, if only I had done this, if only I had done that...this is your life, live in the preciousness of this moment, and treat each person that you meet as a dear friend. The poet Henley wrote, "It matters not how straight the gate, how charged with punishments the scroll, I am the master of my fate, the captain of my soul..." Live your Truth in Light and Joy! NAMASTE.

MEDITATION IN SPIRIT

©1999 KARYN K. MITCHELL, PH.D, N.D.

Please play soft music in the background, relax and enjoy.

It is sunset. As you step from your doorway out into the world around you, you are aware of the vibrant colors of the setting sun...the gold, the terra cotta, the turquoise. As you breathe in the freshness of the air around you, allow your body to relax and become one with the deep sense of freedom that envelopes you. Breathe in peace, and breathe out light. Let go of all your thoughts and concerns about your day. Let them go.

You become aware that you are walking on a path. The path looks very familiar to you, as it represents your life up to this time in your present incarnation. Notice if it is rocky or smooth, wide or narrow. Just ahead of you on the path you notice a building. This building might be a house, a mansion, a castle, a barn, a museum, a library, or any other type of building that appears in your consciousness. How old is this building? This structure represents all lifetimes prior to this one. The door is open and you know that you are to enter in, and you do so with the feelings of reverence and confidence. As you enter, look first to the right of this structure. Be aware of any pictures, furniture, or whatever else might be there. Find an object that belonged to you in your last lifetime. Hold it in your hand and ask your heart this question, "What was most important for me then?" Or, "What was the purpose of that lifetime?" Take a few moments and listen as your heart communicates with you anything that you need to know about that lifetime. Just ahead of you see a stairway that leads up to the next level. As you place your foot upon the first step, you become aware that these are golden steps, seven golden steps that will take you to your Planners. If you wish to meet them, ascend slowly with me, 1-2-3-4-5-6, and at 7 you step off onto the floor In this higher place. There ahead of you is a large table, and behind the table are standing your Planners. How many are there? Ask if you can meet them, and take a few moments to do so, asking their names if they will share them with you. Then ask them why you have chosen to be born into your present lifetime. What is your Soul's Purpose? You may even ask them why you chose your parents in this lifetime. Take some time and communicate with your Planners about your concerns in this life. (Pause)

Before you leave, ask your planners for Spiritual Wisdom. If it is appropriate for you to have it, they will share with you Wisdom that will help you gain a greater understanding of your mission. (Pause) When it is time, you return to the golden steps and descend them slowly and thoughtfully. Each step represents a deeper awareness of the Path: 7.) All life is One 6.) Nurture Life 5.) Share Compassion 4.) Love Others 3.) Love Yourself 2.) Live in Peace 1.) Simplify Your Life. As you step onto the floor, you see the other side of the building, empty and waiting. It represents your future. You have the opportunity to create your future to cultivate the Wisdom that the Planners shared with you. Create your future in that space if it serves your Highest Good. Sense that it is happening. When you are finished, come back through the doorway, out into the rising sun of a new day. The air is fresh and you are renewed. Come back on your path to this moment. Take three deep breaths and return to your home in the now.

Thai Shan
Ming dynasty

Karyn K. Mitchell, N.D., Ph.D.
Biography

Karyn Mitchell is a Naturopathic Doctor with a Ph.D in Psychology. She has attended The University of Iowa, The University of Nebraska, Loras College, Buena Vista College, Midwest University, and Westbrook. She is an international teacher and speaker in the fields of Reiki, Hypnotherapy, Vegetarian Lifestyle, Meditation, Natural Medicine, and Shamanism. She has been a student of Psychology, Metaphysics, Religion, and Philosophy for over thirty years. She is a member of the American Naturopathic Medical Association. She has taken the Five Mindfulness Trainings with Master Thich Nhat Hanh, a Buddhist Monk ordained in the Zen tradition, and has taken initiations and studied with His Holiness the Dalai Lama. Also, Karyn is a graduate of the Silva Method, and has studied Shamanism with Michael Harner and Sandra Ingerman (The Foundation for Shamanic Studies). She has studied other cultural dimensions of Shamanism in other countries and from other instructors. She is a medical intuitive and mystic dedicated to sharing the spirit of compassion and love for people, animals, plants, and minerals.

She is a Holistic Counselor and a Certified Reiki Master-Teacher of the Usui Shiki Ryoho School of Reiki. She is certified through the American Board of Hypnotherapy as an Instructor of Metaphysical Hypnotherapy, and is an instructor certified by the International Medical Dental Hypnotherapy Association (I.M.D.H.A.), and the American Association of Behavioral Therapists. Karyn holds further certification from the National Association for Transpersonal Psychology in the areas of Clinical Hypnotherapy, Transpersonal Therapy, Analytical Hypnotherapy, and Past Life Regression Therapy. She and her husband, Steven Mitchell have co-founded A.R.T., the Association for Regression Therapists, and "Reiki Path" School of Reiki Instruction. They have both devoted their life's work to assisting others with their spiritual growth. Karyn maintains an office at Haven Holistic Center in St. Charles, Illinois and works as a Holistic Counselor, Naturopath, Reiki Practitioner, Teacher, and Regression Therapist. She has taught at three Universities in the United States. Her personal spiritual philosophy is to guide students and clients to a place of personal awareness and empowerment.

Her books, <u>REIKI A TORCH IN DAYLIGHT</u>, <u>REIKI BEYOND THE USUI SYSTEM</u>, and <u>REIKI MYSTERY SCHOOL</u>, published by Mind Rivers, are available through most book stores.

Guided Meditation Tapes

To Order: Call 815-732-7150 with M/C or Visa number or send check to Mind Rivers Publishing, 924 N Daysville, Oregon, IL 61061

Most tapes approximately 50 minutes in length, $10.00 EachPostage Paid in U.S.

REIKI TAPES AVAILABLE:

What Is Reiki?/ Reiki Meditation:
   What Reiki is and does, Precepts and Principles of Reiki. Side two is a meditation.
Experience Reiki.
   How a Reiki Treatment might feel as each chakra is brought into harmony. Experiential.
Absentee Healing/Self Healing:
   Level II practitioners & up. Techniques for self & Absentia Healing.
Vertical Reiki.
   (Two Volume Set $20.) Meditations & Healing with Client Standing. Master Usui's Method Without a Table.
Meeting the Grand Masters:
   Advanced Spiritual Journey to meet Usui, Hayashi, & Takata.

SPIRITUAL ADVANCEMENT TAPES:

Meditation for Spiritual Advancement:
   The next step. A quantum leap in spiritual growth.
Soul Star Meditation/Soul Beyond the River:
   Anchoring energies in the chakra beyond the crown center; Finding the first you to incarnate upon planet Earth..
Journey to the Tao Chakra/Moving Into Light:
   From the Crown to the Soul Star to the "Tao" Chakra, the golden center. Ever dreamed of being pure Light?
Finding Your Soul's Purpose:
   Why have you chosen to be born at this time? Meet special guides.
Depossession as Therapy:
   Based on the Unquiet Dead by Edythe Fiore. Recognize symptoms, & release energies.
Gentle Depossession.
   For therapists & Healers. Karyn Mitchell's technique for releasing energies.
The Emerald, The Eagle, The River, & You.
   Advanced mystical meditation with much symbolism.
Find Your Spirit Guides:
   A tape to help you meet those Guides and Masters who help you.
Healing Your Past:
   A life Regression to heal pain & trauma in the present. Inner Child work.
Past Life Regression As Therapy:
   What it is, how it heals. A regression is included.
Advanced Past Life Techniques:
   The Destiny Train & Portrait Gallery, for groups or individuals.

Atlantis, Lemuria & Space: Regression to the life before your Earth
     Journey.
Abductions: How, When, & Why?
     Tape based on a workshop Karyn teaches throughout the U.S. (The
     Book, ABDUCTIONS, STOP THEM, HEAL THEM, NOW is
     $9.95)
Past Life Relationships:
     Find a present love in a past life.
White Light Cobalt Tetrahedran/Two Invocations
          White Light-InterdimensionalJourney to gain the Cosmic
          Tetrahedran for protection. Two Invocations for healing dis-ease
          and releasing fear.
Interdimensional Chakra Meditation/ Interdimensional Journey
     Journey through the Interdimensional Chakras.
Healing the Child Within:
     Heal your wounded child, and learn what secrets this child holds for
     you.
A Bridge of Light and Transition
     The dying Process and beyond.

HEALING TAPES:

Asthma:
     Three emotional reasons for asthma, and how to heal them.
Smoking Cessation:
     Three strong meditations for freedom from smoking.
Weight Reduction:
     How to achieve and maintain your ideal weight by healing the root
     cause of the situation.
Ayurvedic Weight:
     Based on the book PERFECT WEIGHT by Deepak Chopra. Body
     types & balance techniques
Soul Retrieval:
     Shamanic & Hypnotherapy techniques for restoring the whole soul.
Cancer & Chemotherapy:
     If this is the course of action chosen, then ease the pain of "conven-
     tional treatment".
Healing the Heart
     Meditations for coronary healing & stress release.
Healing the Cells of the Body:
     Using Light, color, and the River of Ki to flow through the body for
     healing.
Chakra Health:
     Cleansing the Chakras and fill them with energy from the Highest
     Light. Spin/open chakras. Grounding.
NOTE: ALL TAPES ARE CREATED & COPYRIGHTED BY KARYN
MITCHELL. MUST NOT BE DUPLICATED OR COPIED.

Other Books Written by
Karyn K. Mitchell N.D., Ph.D

Reiki A Torch In Daylight
ISBN 0-9640822-1-7
Retail $14.95

Reiki: Beyond the Usui System
ISBN 0-9640822-2-5
Retail $19.96

Reiki Mystery School
Transformational Reiki
ISBN 0-9640822-5-X
Retail $19.98

Karyn and Steven Mitchell travel and teach Reiki, TransReiki™, Advanced Reiki Techniques, Hypnotherapy, and Melody Crystal Healing throughout the world. For speaking and teaching engagements, please contact:
Steven Mitchell
815-732-7150
e-mail: mitchell@essex1.com

The Sacred Truth

"*No one knew how long the Order had existed or where it had come from. Some say that its origins paralleled the Christian Biblical Text of The Garden of Eden, only with a far different conclusion. They were freed of the bondage of limited thought and action. Of the original sanctuary, only dusty mantle stones, greatly cracked with age remained near the river's edge. Where the gnarled Tree of Life anchored solid soil in the fertile delta grass above the mud line, marked sacred ground where the seventy-two plus three gathered at sunrise and sunset for their daily rituals and passionate adoration to their one Sun. It was here, on this vibrant life-filled spring evening that the Ancient Mother, Anamnesis, daughter of Sophia, spoke...just as she had for as long as their collective history could remember...*"

The Sacred Truth relates the mystical history of the origins of a hidden religious sect known as the Essenes and the Gnostic Gospels as revealed by an American woman. A spiritual experience leads her to the revelation that she lived more than 6,000 years before Christ, and is the reincarnated granddaughter of the Gnostic Matriarch, Sophia.

These two stories are intricately woven into a spiritual odyssey that transcends space and time and leads us eventually to the First Principle, the author of the Original Gospel, the Sacred Truth, and reveals our way home to the Light. A truly spiritual romance with life.

Comig Soon!! Ask your favorite bookstore to order it for you.

The Sacred Truth